SoJourn

Volume 2, Number 2

A journal devoted to the history, culture, and geography of South Jersey

SJCHC

South Jersey Culture & History Center

Winter 2017–2018

SoJourn is a collaborative effort. Local historians contribute the articles; Stockton students—in this issue, the editing interns of fall 2017—edit the articles, set the type, and design the layout; the directors of the South Jersey Culture & History Center at Stockton University oversee the publication.

Editors
Mallory A. Caignon, Taylor Cills, Emma E. Corcodilos, Kristen M. DeLeonard, Dakota R. DeMarco, Kourtney Gush, Jean Hodges, Amy N. Krieger, Jennifer R. Liebowitz, Kent Mattia, Angela J. Mazzara, Diondra K. Meningall-Burney, Rebecca L. Muller, Evan T. Osborne-Lomax, Kristin A. Robertson, Medgina A. Saint-Elien, Kimberly Santana, Julie A. Scully, Kat H. Wentzell.

Supervising Editors
Tom Kinsella and Paul W. Schopp

ISSN: 2474-6665

ISBN-13: 978-1-947889-99-6

A publication of the South Jersey Culture & History Center
at Stockton University
www.stockton.edu/sjchc/

Filler images, at the conclusion of articles, courtesy of the Paul W. Schopp Collection unless otherwise noted.

To contact SJCHC write:
SJCHC / School of Arts & Humanities
Stockton University
101 Vera King Farris Drive
Galloway, New Jersey
08205

Email:
Thomas.Kinsella@stockton.edu
Paul.Schopp@stockton.edu

About this Issue of *SoJourn*

If well-written articles on local history interest you, I encourage you to peruse this issue of *SoJourn*, our fourth. It continues Stockton University's long-term efforts to explore our South Jersey region through compelling articles, photo essays, and stories. Dip into these pages and you will find readable, well-researched, and (we believe) entertaining accounts. Here are brief descriptions:

- Mary Jo Kietzman traces the deep roots of the Wescoat and Southard families in and around Batsto, Pleasant Mills, and, especially, Nesco. Kietzman explores the relationship between familial identity and place—in this case, the farming community that nurtured several generations of her forebears.
- Hal Taylor follows with an essay that reveals the connections between a Frenchman, a dog, a bottle of brandy, and George Washington. Taylor describes how all are related to the first manned air flight in North America.
- Albertine Senske enables readers to share the beauty of Elizabeth C. White's famed Pine Barrens garden at Whitesbog. The excellent photography of botanist and Pine Barrens historian Ted Gordan visually enhances Albertine's detailed description of White's gardening aesthetic.
- John Lawrence follows the twists and turns of history- and myth-making that took a brief entry in early Dutch explorer David de Vries' journal, one that succinctly detailed his 1633 interaction with an unnamed Lenni-Lenape woman, and expanded it into Romantic accounts with slight historical foundation; the accounts tell more about the perspectives of nineteenth-century historians than events along the Delaware in the seventeenth-century.
- Rich Watson takes readers in search of the ghost town of Calico, near Martha Furnace, and, in so doing, offers readers an insightful study of Pine Barrens land use over time.
- Claude Epstein provides readers with a brief history of waterborne diseases in South Jersey, as well as a detailed description of the governmental structures, processes, and technologies that evolved to fight harmful pollutants.
- Amy Krieger, a Literature major at Stockton, welcomes Stockton's new Special Collections Librarian and Archivist, Heather Perez, in an article that also briefly describes the South Jersey collections held at Stockton University's Bjork Library.

- Atlantic white cedar is the star of the article by our colleagues at the Rutgers University Marine Field Station. Following its growth over time, including its longevity as Ghost Forests, provides an excellent method to discern sea-level rise.
- The issue closes with two linked short stories by Dallas Lore Sharp, describing a spring freshet along the Maurice River. Lore reminds us in spellbinding prose that spring is coming.

We hope you enjoy these articles. Please remember that we are always seeking contributing authors for future issues.

Tom Kinsella

Director
South Jersey Culture & History Center
Stockton University

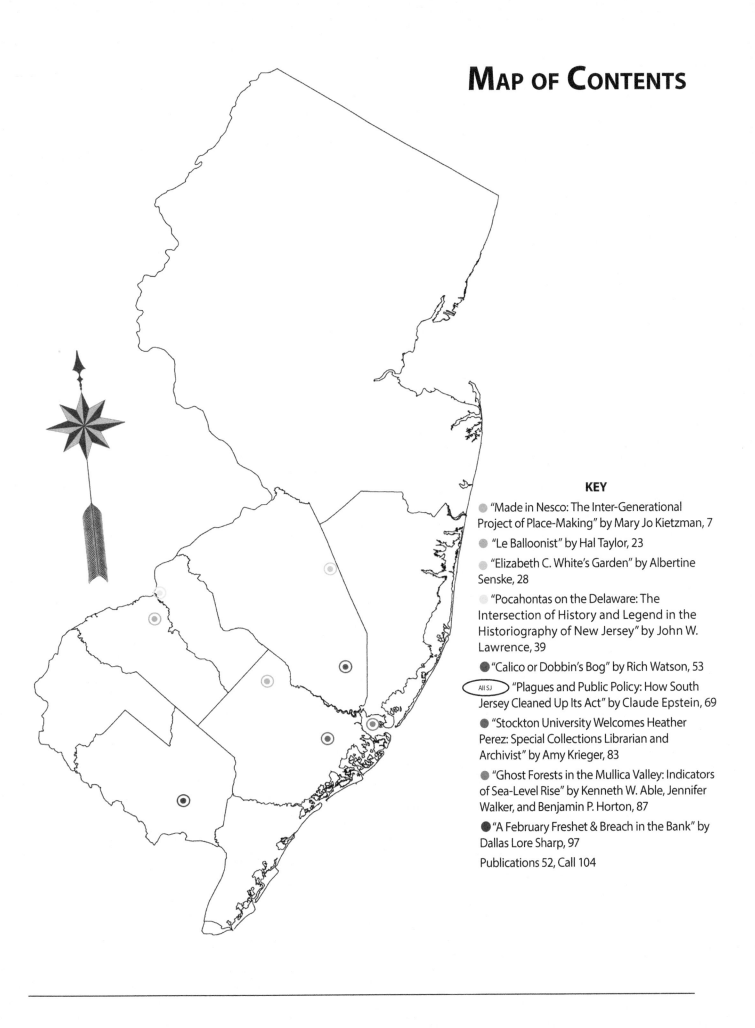

Map of Contents

KEY

CHART OF DELAWARE BAY, 1850

Born in 1770, Edmund March Blunt grew to become one of America's first hydrographers (*hydrography* is the science of surveying and charting bodies of water). During 1796, Blunt produced his first edition of the *American Coast Pilot*. This published work provided the masters of coastal schooners with detailed sailing directions along the east coast from Passamaquoddy, Maine, to the Strait of Florida. In addition to his printed directions, his books contained folded chart plates for the ocean and navigable rivers and streams. These charts featured soundings (depth of water) in fathoms (six feet=one fathom), bearings to lighthouses or other tall structures, along with denoting the locations of rocks, shoals, ledges, etc. Course and distance tables, current tables, and tide tables completed the volume.

The *American Coast Pilot* went through 21 editions with a new edition issued every two to three years. Edmund's son, George William Blunt, joined with his father in the publishing work after reaching his majority. When Edmund died in 1862, George continued producing new editions of the *American Coast Pilot* with the twenty-first edition published in 1867. After Blunt released this edition, the United States Coast and Geodetic Survey negotiated with George to acquire the rights to continue publishing the work and the National Oceanic and Atmospheric Administration, successor to the coast & geodetic survey, still publishes this valuable guide to navigation.

The Delaware Bay chart reproduced here is from the sixteenth edition of the *American Coast Pilot,* published in 1850. Produced with a copper plate engraved in reverse by a C. Copley, the intaglio printing is obvious as you run your finger lightly over the chart's surface and feel the raised ink. Not only is there plenty of detail here for mariners, but also for historians. The number of labeled toponyms is surprising throughout the chart and places like Lannings Wharf, Beaden's Cove, and Robinson's Beach are seldom found on other cartographic sources. For durability, the chart is printed on 100 percent cotton rag paper, allowing the folded map to be opened and refolded numerous time without wearing out or separating at the fold.

Paul W. Schopp

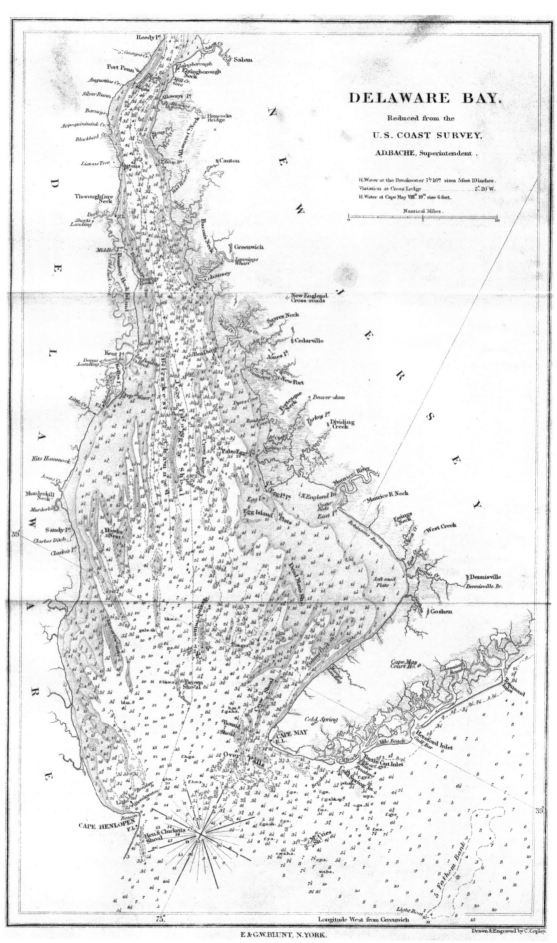

DELAWARE BAY.

Reduced from the

U.S. COAST SURVEY,

A.D. BACHE, Superintendent.

H. Water at the Breakwater 7ʰ 16ᵐ rises 5 feet 10 inches.
Variation at Cross Ledge   2° 20′ W.
H. Water at Cape May VIIIʰ 19ᵐ rise 6 feet.

Nautical Miles.

E. & G.W. BLUNT, N. YORK.

Drawn & Engraved by C. Copley.

Made in Nesco:
The Inter-Generational Project of Place-Making

Mary Jo Kietzman

"Glens Falls never felt like home. It was just a place to live," she says dragging on a Kool cigarette, deep into her reminiscences about the place that *did* feel like home—Nesco, a settlement west of Batsto, on the edge of the Pine Barrens in southern New Jersey. She has just finished demonstrating how the rusted contraption—a tape dispenser for packing blueberries—works. She rescued it from the cellar and put down her cigarette long enough to show me on an imaginary pint how she would hold the cellophane with one hand and tape it down with the other. She was nine years old when she began packing blueberries for her uncle Philip and would pack thousands more every summer until she was 23. She's 86 now. Her hands look more natural than human—rocks and roots under fragile skin that bruises easily. She blames the arthritis in her hands on packing blueberries, which required the same motion for countless hours. But she energetically recalls getting up at 6:00 every morning during blueberry season and racing out to the packing shed in order to pack more pints than her competitor, Elmira. On one trip back home, we sat in the parking lot of the HoJo's on the

Wescoat family house. *All images courtesy of the author.*

White Horse Pike (all the ancestral houses have been sold) smoking, watching heat lightning, and talking to some guys selling equipment to blueberry farmers. She told them that in her heyday she could pack 5,000 pints a day. "That's as fast as our machines," they said dubiously, but I believed her. After all, I'd grown up on these stories in which Mom, Catherine Alice (Midge) Walker Kietzman, was always the hero and the work she did—more of and better than anyone else—"never felt like work exactly." She milked cows, cultivated fields, scooped cranberries, picked strawberries, packed blueberries, went clamming on the bay and sold the clams door to door in Nesco. But her stories also introduced me to a large family—my family—Wescoats and Southards, Wares, Gaskells, Abbots, Petersons, Landys, and Fords—all of whom lived up and down Pleasant Mills Road and worked together in the cranberry bogs, berry fields, and in the small truck farm. I knew and loved my grandparents, Lillian and Frank, and my great uncle, Philip, and his wife, Ruth. But even those who had died—Philip Wescoat ("Grampy"), Catherine Southard, Philip's brothers, and Catherine's siblings sprang to vivid life in

From left: Frank Walker, Mary Southard Birdsall, Catherine Southard Wescoat, Mary's daughter Katie, Lillian Wescoat Walker, Philip Wescoat, posed before Frank's Ford Model A, circa 1930.

the tales my mother would tell. I felt myself to be on intimate terms with them, just as I did with the characters in the fiction I devoured laying on the settee on Grandmother's side porch.

My early life was lived on car rides between South Jersey and upstate New York—between flatlands where the sea air permeates even the pine woods and the foothills of the Adirondacks. There was no question which world was more vital to me. Sitting in the passenger seat, gazing across the sandy soil of blueberry fields one last time before getting on the Jersey Turnpike north, I wanted to stay in Nesco. Barring that, I knew how to ask the questions that would lead my mother to open her past. And so I listened. And I remembered. I was the good daughter. But there was more to it. Even as a very young girl, I sensed that her stories about the ancestors and her need to repeat place names was an essential activity that kept Nesco, and all it represented, alive. As one highway led to another, my clear prospect into the past closed. Suddenly, we were back "home," stranded in a cramped Cape Cod far from the shore—the rooms boringly geometric—where I had the recurring fantasy that if the house were a boat crashing into an iceberg, the four upstairs bedrooms would split into quarters like the grilled cheese sandwiches Mom would carefully cut for us. It was never clear what held

suburbia together or even my particular nuclear family. Nesco was different. There the affiliations were written on the landscape in the gathering of dwellings and outbuildings. Each one had a distinct character that expressed its purpose, but they stood together because this family, which was also a community, was busy making and growing things.

The farmstead Grampy built (with beams from the Batsto schoolhouse) was at the center of Nesco (as I knew it), consisting of a house, two barns, a brick fruithouse, icehouse, and the only brick privy in Nesco. Grampy is my great-grandfather, Philip Wescoat (1869–1947), the first farmer to grow blueberries in the area of Hammonton—a town that, today, declares itself "the Blueberry Capitol of the World."[1] When his daughter, Lillian, who taught in the one-room school at Weekstown, married Frank Walker from Tansboro, Grampy gave her 33 acres of oaks across the road and built her a stately white house. Next to Lillian was Uncle Harry Wescoat, who owned and operated the sawmill that made the crates for cranberries and later blueberries. Philip's wife, Catherine Southard, had relatives along the same stretch of road: Frank Southard, Charlie Southard and Aunt Nelly. Nesco, historians say, was named for the Nescochague Indians, but in the past, it had been called by various other names: "New Columbia," "Wescoatville," "Wescoat's Neck" and "Wescoat Landing." This is fitting, since Grampy's grandfather, William Westcoat, ran a glass-making factory, store, and tavern just down the road near the intersection of the present-day Columbia Road. William's son, David, was a collier (charcoal maker) as well as a carpenter who also grew blackberries. Five generations before I arrived, the settlement that felt like my home was a much more industrious place than I could guess. Peter Wacker, geographer of early New Jersey, notes the importance of agglomerated settlements (clustered residences with cultural centers like church and school); but he is, I think, mistaken to suggest that rural life was dispersed.[2] It was not that way in Nesco, where families stuck together and cooperated to make a thriving community organized around industries. "It's still that way," insisted my cousin Dave Ware at a recent meeting of Wescoat descendants at the local history museum ("Mullica in the Pines"), housed in the Hilda Frame four-room schoolhouse on Pleasant Mills Road. "If somebody needs a roof, we get together and put a roof on." My aunt, uncle, and cousins spoke of a much larger array of local industries that included gathering pinecones and sphagnum moss as well as cutting cattails at places called Marigold and Mud Point. They all embrace the Piney identity that, to them, means living off the land in a tightly knit, if not quite inbred, community.

Nesco was not an anomaly; it had prototypes. The original agglomerated community in the area was The Forks, a general place name that embraced not only the island landing in the Mullica River, but the village of Pleasant Mills. The Forks was developed in the 1750s as a center of trade. To avoid duties at the Port of Philadelphia, goods were shipped up the Mullica, navigable by seafaring ships, offloaded onto wagons, and hauled overland through the Pines to Camden and Philadelphia. Colonel Richard Wescoat, who had a house and tavern at The Forks, oversaw this trade and became wealthy enough from it to purchase Elijah Clark's plantation, which included the landing (shipyard), a sawmill and grist mill, a dwelling house (the "Kate Aylesford" mansion), barn, stables, out-houses, a blacksmith shop, wet and dry goods stores, and houses for workmen and tradesmen—"indeed every building necessary and convenient for carrying on business and trade extensively, for which the situation of the place is exceedingly well calculated, both by nature and improvement."[3] Richard was the eldest son of Daniel and Deborah Wescoat, and it was his younger brother, Thomas—my ancestor—who moved up Pleasant Mills Road to establish Wescoatville or Nesco.

Batsto may have been an even more important prototype for Nesco. It began with a sawmill when Richard Wescoat purchased property at a foreclosure sale by the Common Pleas Court in 1764. One year later, Wescoat sold a half-interest in the property to Charles Read, who understood, after surveying the availability of resources, that this was the ideal place for an ironworks. It was Read who dammed the Batsto River and erected Batsto Furnace in 1766.[4] When Philadelphia merchant and trader, John Cox—"among the more active and ardent yet lesser known patriots of the American Revolution"—bought into the venture, Batsto began producing a wide variety of commercial and household articles—iron pots, kettles, dutch ovens—as well as the usual pig iron and, crucially, cannonballs and musket balls for Washington's army.[5] Joseph Ball took over as manager at Batsto in 1776 and became primary owner of the ironworks three years later. The financial experience of running the furnace served him well as director of the First Bank of United States and president of the Insurance Company of North America. Batsto continued to prosper through the War of 1812 until new methods of smelting, which used coal instead of charcoal, gave Pennsylvania iron and steel a competitive edge. But even after its ironmaking days were over, Jesse Richards built a glasshouse that began production in 1846, and, for over twenty years, Batsto supplied window glass and the panes for gas lights to Camden, Philadelphia and New York. In Batsto, with its furnace, gristmill, sawmill, post office, company store, workers' cottages (65 homes are found in a 1854 list), and ironmaster's house, there was no question that community and industry were integrated from the start.

In his book, *Forging America*, John Bezis-Selfa argues that the early iron industry generated an "industrious revolution," in which work was perceived as a route to economic independence and even political power. Evidence from New Jersey, however, leads him to acknowledge that industriousness was situated in tight communities, and that forges or furnaces could be nearly "self-contained worlds." In a description of his visit to Lancaster County's Mount Hope Furnace in 1799, Polish statesman Julian Ursyn Niemcewicz emphasized values of community over those of industry, "Attached as they are to the place on which a large number of them were born . . . these people keep their place" and, evidently, understood their relationship to the ironmaster as a reciprocal one in the service of shared goals.[6] Historian Charles Boyer maintains that slaves did not produce Batsto iron as was the case in many North Jersey furnaces. He describes the relations between the ironmasters, particularly William Richards, and the workers as "feudal": "He was not only the friend of those employed at the furnace and on the farms, but also their counselor," providing doctors, lawyers, ministers when needed, houses at nominal rents, and credit for all at the company store.[7] But Richards' Quakerism seems to me to be an important factor that historians have overlooked. Quakers believed that every person contained the divine light, and they addressed one another, regardless of class affiliation, with the nominative "thou." So it stands to reason that their social relations would be egalitarian and their bonds reciprocal—even covenantal.

I didn't know this stuff intellectually on those car rides with my mother, but I knew that a whole world and a significant way of life was being lost when she uprooted herself. I also knew that her storytelling and now my storytelling are a form of place-making or place sensing. "What people make of their places," writes anthropologist Keith Basso, "is closely connected to what they make of themselves as members of society and inhabitants of the earth."[8] Wisdom sits in places. I'd like to think that my mother knew this as well as any of the Apache wise men Basso interviews. I'd like to think that the hours spent talking story about the places around Nesco and what happened in them were efforts to transfer wisdom to her children, giving us tools for living. But this may be my own wishful thinking.

Closer to truth, perhaps, is that my mother, like all transplants, was withering out of her element. J. D. Vance documents this process for his hillbilly grandparents,

who moved from western Kentucky to the steel mills of Middletown, Ohio, for work.[9] My mother didn't leave home until she was 30 because the family relied on her labor, and she was teaching school with her mother, who had moved from the one-room schoolhouse in Weekstown to a four-room building in Elwood.[10] The ostensible motive for her move north was recreational: she'd watched the 1956 Olympics and, excited by the idea of skiing, she joined the Jersey Skeeters and made week-end trips to Gore Mountain in her '57 Chevy. She also got sick. Lying in a hospital bed with septicemia from an ovarian cyst, a teacher-friend of her mother's told her that if she didn't leave home, she'd never get married. My mother left to have her own individual life and pursue her own dream of happiness; these pursuits are, after all, part of the American narrative inflected differently in each generation. But as she moved forward alone, the concomitant experience (as it is, I think, for many Americans) is a homesickness that runs deep.[11] Despite the rented apartment next door to Glens Falls High School, where she was a star teacher, despite the fun she had with Baron Fitzgerald in North Creek, despite getting a date with the guy who drove a T-bird around town, the proverbial grains of Jersey sand in her shoes were more like seeds out of which grew her Nesco mythology.

"What bothered me about my family was that they never did anything," she says, thinking about her own nuclear family and confusing me because what she says is not objectively true. Her father, Frank, was a boiler

Wescoat Jersey cows.

inspector on the railroad, and her mother, Lillian, taught in a one-room schoolhouse and became the principal of the consolidated Elwood school. At her funeral, a former student described "Mrs. Walker" as "an institution." But my mother's comment speaks to the fact that neither Lillian nor Frank were farmers, and Mom loved farm work. For her, farm work was not drudgery but a practice—not unlike a carpenter's or a mason's craft—that connected her to fields, bogs, barns, and Grampy.[12] She knew the personalities of the cows she milked every morning and evening, and, in her eyes, each blueberry had a face.

Migration to upstate New York probably magnified the significance of Nesco for my mother, and my imagination did the rest. To me, Mom—"riding her horse through the peach orchard"—was a cross between Willa Cather's Antonia and Thomas Hardy's Tess, and Grampy was to Nesco what Adam was to Eden: he tilled the soil, sustained life, and rested on the seventh day.[13] "On summer Sundays, we packed up Grampy's seven-passenger Packard, loaded with food and even a table. There was a luggage rack on the back. And we'd head out to Brigantine." But work wasn't the sole criteria for entry into the Nesco Hall of Fame. Hazel Landy was there, too, with the distinction of having breasts so large they got caught in the wringers of a washing machine. And Mom often told stories about Frank Southard—"Uncle Tinky"—who'd get "drunk as a lord" and with whom she'd "talk over the problems of the world." Marriage changed everything. My mother, the heroic worker and gifted storyteller, was yoked to a man who "didn't talk much" and wound up housebound in suburbia, hosting coffee get-togethers for neighborhood women and raising four little kids. I have come to understand her mythology as a lifeline to a time when she "did things"—when she and her brother were "the worst kids in Nesco," tipping over outhouses and jumping off barn roofs with umbrellas, and when she was the star of the high school basketball team, Eat-Mor cranberry queen, and champion blueberry packer.

Her hero stories spoke of a community in which no one was anonymous; each man, woman, boy and girl had a big personality and could potentially bend the world, or a piece of it anyway, to his or her will. Many of her relatives did just that. Though influenced by Mom's mythology, my Nesco story will be more a study, more an ethnography of a way of life that contains the imaginative raw material for a new version of an American dream of the individual in community, who is free—not to do anything she wants—but free in that she is educated and encouraged to play a public role and contribute to a common collaborative project.

PANTHEON

> When I was about five years old, recovering from measles, my grandfather came into my room, pulled me out of bed and held me up at the window. "Look at that!" he said, and I saw a dirigible hovering in the sky with a swastika on the tail fin. "We'll be at war with them soon," he said, and he was right. He knew things.

Uncle Bud tells me this story over the phone. All of his memories of growing up in Nesco, like my mother's, swirl around the tremendous character of Grampy; and in them, I hear echoes of a child's love, respect, and awe. "I worked with Grampy all my life," says Mom, "and when he died, he was laid out in the parlor of Gran's house. I had to vacuum around the casket, and I talked to him. But it drove me crazy that I could never say what he was like." Oral cultures, as literary historian Walter Ong reminds us, do not conceptualize and verbalize their knowledge through elaborate analytic categories at a distance from lived experience.[14] My mother's Nesco retained many features of an oral society.

Although Grampy had enough education to effectively run businesses, his son, Philip, had only a sixth-grade education. It was the Wescoat women who gained and valued literacy; and the mother root seems to have been Ellen Flood, an Irish immigrant who came to America alone (probably in the 1860s) and worked as a servant in the Batsto mansion during the tenure of one of the Richards' heirs.[15] Her daughter, Catherine Southard, although born at Batsto, worked in the book department of Wanamaker's department store in Philadelphia, possibly commuting to work by train. Catherine's daughter, Lillian Wescoat, went to Glassboro Normal School; and her daughters, Catherine (Midge) and Ruthellen, graduated from Georgian Court College in Lakewood, New Jersey, and the University of Miami, respectively.[16]

With a foot in both oral and literate worlds, my mother's way of understanding her grandfather was to remember their shared labor. My way of working her question, "what was Grampy like?" is to see him in the context of his own time and as one in a sequence of Wescoat men all of whom were resourceful projectors.

What impresses me the most is that these men did not learn a single trade or specialize in a single crop (as people tend to do today); their industries were varied and experimental. Blueberry farming was, for instance, a natural outgrowth of cranberry culture, because "the plants are genetically very close and require the same basic conditions except cranberries are wet and blueberries are dry" explains the historian Jeff Macechak,

Outreach Coordinator at the Burlington County Historical Society. Grampy was 56 years old when he began the blueberry venture after seasons when the cranberries were not blighted (as I always heard) but had a "false bloom" ("the vines and flowers looked fine, but there was no fruit"). But even after planting the blueberries, he continued to grow cranberries and other vegetables, run a dairy farm, and operate a mechanic shop and Packard dealership. In sustaining a range of enterprises, he differed from the Italians who, once they got into blueberries in the 1940s, phased out all other crops and made blueberries the local agro-industry.[17] One of Bud's harder-to-believe stories, but one which speaks to the competitive animosity "Yankees" felt toward "blackies," is that after Grampy planted his first quarter-acre of blueberries, Italians came in at night and stole the plants . . . "I had never seen him angry before," notes my uncle. The animosity stemmed from the fact that the Italians worked harder and cheaper than local whites—"they'd walk barefoot from Hammonton to Bulltown."

"With all the land he owned and all Grampy got into," my mother wonders, "how was it that we never seemed to have money? Someone must have really mismanaged." It occurs to me that world-making may have been more important than money-making, and profits were used to seed new industries. Grampy opened the Packard "sub-dealership" in Hammonton in 1924 and my uncle Bud remembers that "one day he went to a dealership in Philadelphia with an order for three automobiles. No one would wait on him because he had holes in his sweater and was wearing hip boots, but when they did, he bought three cars—two to ship overseas and one to drive home in. He may have looked like a bum, but he was "a real gentleman." A gentleman, who even played cricket in his younger days at church picnics in Green Bank.[18]

My mother's impulse to turn people into heroes is important. Sociologist Philip Gorski stresses the importance of a pantheon—a collection of founders, heroes, or saints—in any tradition, because "abstract principles do not always provide an adequate guideline for human conduct. One needs moral exemplars as well, individuals who embodied these principles in their lives and can therefore serve as models of excellence."[19] Histories of early New Jersey single out the patriots, privateers, and ironmasters who stood out—one of them was Colonel Richard Wescoat, and it is with him I'll begin a brief examination of the projecting tendency that may have been partially "genetic," but was more likely produced by the marriage of inventive minds with the variety of Pine Barrens' ecosystems—woods, swamps, rivers, and bay—that offered many opportunities for trade, agriculture, and industry.

Richard Wescoat

Born in 1733 in Bedford, New York, to Deborah and Daniel Wescoat, Richard relocated with the family to The Forks in 1748. Prior familiarity with the region is likely as Richard traveled down the coast and up inland waterways to cut timber for shipment to New York for fuel, lumber, and shingles.[20] Arthur Pierce describes him as a dashing figure, a subject fit for historical novels, and the Wescoat genealogy further characterizes him as "sprightly, fractitious . . . possessing a great share of . . . mother wit" and "inclined to partnerships" with men like Elijah Clark, Charles Read, and John Cox. Wescoat understood the Mullica River's significance as a trade route, linking the sea with cities.[21] Prior to the Revolution, he smuggled goods, and during the war he captured British schooners and sold both the vessels and their contents at The Forks of Little Egg Harbor.

Ships unloaded barrels of sugar and bags of coffee, boxes of tea, puncheons of rum; and the goods, along with iron products and munitions made at Batsto, were hauled overland to Philadelphia, over the old Pine Barrens trails. Pierce notes that there were, along these trails, "many hiding places, with caches for goods in every bog, while loads of salt hay might conceal sugar, molasses, and other contraband."[22] The captured sloops, schooners, and brigs were also auctioned at "Publick Vendue [Sale]," frequently at the house of Richard Wescoat; and these sales were advertised in Pennsylvania and New Jersey newspapers throughout the Revolutionary War. One such advertisement, from the December 18, 1782, *New Jersey Gazette*, itemizes the cargoes of the schooner DOLPHIN and sloop DIAMOND, which were also for sale:

> 300 bushels of coarse salt, 25 barrels of flour, and a pretty large quantity of the following articles, viz. Queen's ware in crates, sorted; cutlery and hard ware in cases, writing paper, playing cards, silk handkerchiefs and ribbons, Irish linens and Britanias, coarse and fine broad cloths, ready made mens clothes, English steel, manufactured mustard, ground ginger in bags.[23]

The Mullica supply line (with landings at Chestnut Neck and The Forks) as well as Batsto Furnace had to be defended from the British. Wescoat volunteered early for the Gloucester County militia, reputedly crossed the Delaware with Washington's army on that snowy Christmas night of 1776, and was wounded at the pivotal battle of Trenton the next day. He recovered, but spent the rest of the war defending the Little Egg Harbor area; militiamen involved in the defense of the Mullica and workers at Batsto were given exemptions from active duty. In 1777, Wescoat, along with Elijah Clark, built a fort at Chestnut Neck at their own expense and outfitted it with cannon to prevent the British from sailing up the Mullica to raid The Forks and burn Batsto, which they attempted on October 6, 1778. Colonial interest and self-interest worked together in Wescoat's career. Tax lists show him owning 60 acres of land in 1773, but by 1784, he owned 500 acres of improved land, 8 horses, 20 horned cattle, 1¼ sawmills, 1 gristmill, 1 tavern, and half a vessel. He purchased the Pleasant Mills plantation in 1779 from Clark and sold it in 1782, anticipating victory for the colonial forces and a dwindling war boom at The Forks. Wescoat also sold his interest in Batsto in 1784, before moving to Mays Landing, where, as Glick's genealogy notes, he "moved all the way," establishing businesses and becoming an important citizen.[24]

WILLIAM WESCOAT

My mother's family descends from Thomas Wescoat, Richard's younger brother. The men in that line moved down the road from The Forks and Batsto to establish their own operations in New Columbia or Nesco. By the 1840s, iron furnaces like Batsto, which burned charcoal and smelted bog ore, were superseded by the anthracite furnaces of Pennsylvania. Jesse Richards, the Batsto ironmaster, was preparing to try glassmaking at Batsto, but he was in serious financial difficulties. Perhaps he sought partnerships as a way of staying solvent, and records show that he deeded William Wescoat (b. 1798) ten acres of land in New Columbia on which he built a glassworks. In partnership with an English glassmaker James M. Brookdale, Wescoat's New Columbia shop was producing glass by 1845—a full year before it was made in Batsto—and by 1851 he had become skilled enough to win a silver medal from the American Institute for the excellent color of his window glass.[25] Near the glasshouse, Wescoat also built a store, a tavern, and ran a stagecoach line; silver plates have been unearthed engraved Wescoat hotel.

Portions of William Wescoat's journal that survive give us a glimpse of the way extended family life built a larger community. There are notations for providing wood for desks and seats to the "Free School," and there is a note about drafting an order to move "the poor house 28 miles from my house." Many Wescoats are named in the register who received foodstuffs and crockery at the store as well as services: shoes and boots were mended, transport arranged, legal counsel provided, coffins made, graves dug, and funerals planned. Payments were accepted in cash, but also in labor—so many days spent chopping wood or working in coal pits.[26]

William and Elizabeth Britton, his wife, had fourteen children, including a son David, born in 1826. Nicknamed "Cockrobin," David was a carpenter by trade as well as a collier who also grew blackberries. William Wescoat sold David for $650 the 22 acres along Pleasant Mills Road that, upon David's death, were parceled out to the relatives I had heard stories about: Charles and Mary Rosell, Harry and Olive Wescoat, Levi Wescoat and his wife, and, of course, Philip Wescoat and Katie Southard.

PHILIP WESCOAT

Grampy exercised his industry and invention in both agricultural and business projects: he was a carpenter who built a farmstead as well as a wooden motor boat; he farmed cranberries and blueberries; he ran a mechanic shop out of his garage and opened a Packard dealership in Hammonton; and he was one of the first land speculators on the island of Brigantine. According to my Uncle Bud, Grampy met Catherine Southard, who lived at Batsto, built a "courting surrey" in his father's blacksmith shop, and married "Kate" in March of 1900. Bud thinks he was doing some kind of farm work for Joseph Wharton, who bought Batsto in 1876 for $14,000. Wharton planned to use the Pine Barrens' aquifer as a water source for Philadelphia, but after the Philadelphia City fathers showed disinterest in the project and local people

American Institute silver medal, awarded to the New Columbia Glass Company, For Window Glass, Best Color, 1851.

objected vociferously, Wharton turned his attention to agriculture, cattle-raising, and cranberry culture.

There are notes in my collection of documents from the Wharton Farm, in which agents offered $1,000 for title to Sleepy Creek, a 23 acre parcel of land in the middle of the Wharton tract that Philip Wescoat owned. The swamp had been in and out of Wescoat hands since 1793, when maps indicate that the land had already been mined for coaling wood and ore. Family oral tradition suggests that it was Grampy's main cranberry bog and that he'd become "pretty good" with dynamite, blasting the stumps out to prepare the bog for farming. Receipts show steady shipments of cranberries by rail to New York and Philadelphia through the 1880s. My mother recalls standing knee-deep in the bog and using a home-made rake of close-set and heavy teeth to comb through the plants to collect the reddening berries. The berries were then dumped into huge wooden vats in the fruit-house, a brick barn built with bricks from the defunct glassworks in Herman City on the Mullica. According to my mother, "Air was blasted into the vats to blow out the plants and sticks that had been scooped out of the bogs with the berries. Then the cranberries would roll down

two wooden chutes. Local women would sit on each side and sort the berries. The good ones would bounce. Then they were transferred to wooden cranberry boxes."

Cranberries were shipped to Philadelphia by train on the West Jersey and Seashore Railroad and to Atlantic City and New York on a boat Grampy made that was powered by a naphtha-fueled engine. The craft looks elegant in the old photos and he also used it to cultivate business relationships. An item in a 1913 newspaper describes a group of bankers from the Peoples Bank boarding Philip Wescoat's boat at Lower Bank and "going down by the inside channel to Atlantic City," where they were met by other important local financiers and "treated to a long automobile ride about the city and suburbs, ending at the hotel where they were to dine." Apparently, the wives showed up at the hotel to surprise their husbands: "The ladies had arranged it and all kept the secret. The united party returned home by the last train in the evening."[27] It is possible that relationships, forged on such pleasure trips, enabled him to procure the necessary loans for the business ventures he began in the next decade on the eve of the '29 crash: a Packard dealership in 1924, cultivated blueberries in 1926, and

Philip Wescoat's naptha launch on the Mullica River.

significant land purchases on the island of Brigantine in 1928.

Grampy got into blueberries ten years after Elizabeth White, daughter of a local cranberry grower, partnered with the botanist Frederick Coville to hybridize native species of huckleberries to produce blueberry plants suitable for cultivation and sale. Experiments began in 1916 when local people were hired to bring back native plants. Invoices preserved in Grampy's old railroad chest show that he began buying blueberry plants (eight different varieties) from Joseph J. White, Inc. in 1926 at 60 cents per plant.[28] Family oral history always claimed that he initially paid $50.00 per plant, and Albertine Senske, the archivist at Whitesbog Preservation Trust, said that the prices could run as high as $25.00 per bush, depending on the size and rarity of the plant. Whitesbog holds the records of Tru-Blu, the first blueberry growers' cooperative, established in 1927. I knew that Grampy belonged to the American Cranberry Growers' Exchange (Eatmor), and it occurred to me that the Tru-Blu records might help me prove whether or not he was the first blueberry farmer in Hammonton. "Oh, no. He wouldn't have joined such a group," insisted Uncle Bud, "he didn't believe in them. He was a loner." But, when I arrived at Whitesbog, Ms. Senske handed me a photocopy of the Tru-Blu minutes for February 14, 1931, and there was his name, "Philip Wescott, Hammonton," approved for membership.[29] At the time, there were only eighteen farmers who belonged to the cooperative, and all of them were in the Pemberton region. "So he *was* the first in Hammonton," I said. "It certainly looks like it," said Albertine, "but the curious thing is that I can't find him anywhere in the records after 1932." So it seems that Bud was right, too. Grampy preferred to go it alone. A growers' cooperative regulated prices, protecting farmers from years when the harvest was poor, but it also prevented them from seeking their own markets and gleaning perhaps greater profits. It takes new bushes about three years to develop a marketable crop. In 1930, Philip Wescoat sold his berries to Tru-Blu for a very small profit ($11.25), but by 1938, my receipts show that he was selling berries directly to produce commission merchants in New York and Philadelphia. Just as his fields were beginning to produce enough fruit to sell, the Depression hit, and prices dropped. Farmers were advised to increase acreage, work on developing yield capacity, and ride it out.[30] By the time I was a child, the Wescoats had close to 200 acres of blueberries, and the family business was in its third generation. The DeMarcos, Bertinos, and Merlinos were still just beginners.

Sensing Place

The idea for the trip began when Mom told me during a phone call that her younger sister, Ruthellen—who ran an antique store in Miami—planned to sell a package of documents, including letters from "Wharton Farm," relating to Sleepy Creek on Ebay. In an effort to make sense of the old deeds and maps, she'd call my mother many times a day and together, both smoking Kools at each end of the line, they'd discuss places with names like Amatol, Meschesetauxen, Totem Village, and Atsion. "I remember it all," she tells me on the phone, "because I worked in those places. Ruthellen doesn't remember because she didn't work there." When I told Mom that I intended to buy the documents, she said predictably, "Oh, Mary Jo, what does it matter?" I understood that documents were far less important than my mother's sense of these places, which still lived in her memory and muscle memory. But the documents mattered to me; and if I had to buy my symbolic birthright, I would. I'd never been to Sleepy Creek, but I'd heard about it all my life. Playing in grandmom's field, there was a swampy patch that we kids crossed by pushing through briars and balancing on a beam sunk in mud. I imagined this was what Sleepy Creek must be like. The swamp symbolized all that was magical and inaccessible about my mother's world. Of course, I won the auction. I was the only bidder, despite my aunt's conviction that someone from the Wharton School of Business would bid on them. The deeds and small maps folded to fit into a pocket were fascinating, but what I really wanted was my mother to teach me the significance of these places. I proposed that she and I, with my young daughter and my younger sister, take a summer road trip back home. Although the premise of the trip was to go to Sleepy Creek, along the way I hoped to record my mother's stories about these places.

"It's been years, but the way we always went to Sleepy Creek was the road behind the church at Batsto."

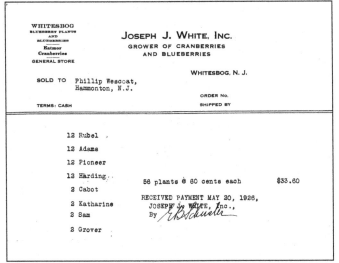

Joseph J. White, Inc. Invoice for sale of blueberry plants to Philip Wescoat, 1926.

We pull into the Pleasant Mills cemetery. It's all sand and cedars with a tea-colored stream winding around the perimeter. This amber water, with the scent and savor of the cedars upon it, has had the reputation of having so lasting a sweetness that it does not grow foul or flat during a long sea voyage. The bridge looks like it has been out for generations. It may be passable on foot, but there is no way for a car to cross. Instead, we wander the paths and through the high grass as we visit the generations of Wescoats and Southards, whose headstones stand companionably side by side in sunlight, keeping their place, as they had done since the 1760s. It is warm and very peaceful with the insects humming and lizards zipping across lichen-encrusted markers. "Death is part of life," my mother has always said. But I only feel the wisdom of her saying here, where our ancestors rest so close to the tidal Mullica, which brings the rise and fall of the sea inland. The sand here is the color and texture of beach sand. I pick up a smooth white pebble, let go of my fixation on Sleepy Creek, and we get into the car and go back down to Nesco to look at the houses where my mother was born and raised.

It seemed inevitable that we'd go to Grampy's first. From a distance, we see a modern looking woman trotting out to pour chemicals into an above-ground pool. She didn't bother us as we did a walking tour of the property: icehouse, fruit house, privy, chicken coop, and barn (with its familiar cool and musky smell of animals and time). My sister Jenny insists that we knock on the door, introduce ourselves, and go in. I can tell that Mom is reluctant, but we do. I hear her repeat family stories to the woman, whose husband is a psychologist in far away Berlin, New Jersey, and we walk through the reconfigured rooms as if in a dream. Mom remembers Gran (Catherine Wescoat) sitting in the parlor alcove saying her rosary—"that was when she was an old woman," and the blond woman says that a previous owner was sure that there was a ghost in the house whose name was Catherine. I later learned from Uncle Bud that the previous owner "described my grandmother exactly, getting all the details right—shoes, apron, bonnet." Eventually, we make our way across the street, and walk through grandmother's house. The owner is a Ford descendant—a distant relation with deep roots at Batsto, but this woman works as a librarian in Laurel Springs. Nesco, it seems, has become a pleasant country get-away for white-collar workers who live elsewhere. I have to laugh as I recall reading in Cornelius Weygandt's *Down Jersey*, published in 1940, an old-timer's diagnosis of the cultural problem: "it ain't right to have the schools usening the children to soft jobs. That's most what's the matter with the country now, soft jobs."[31]

In both houses, walls have been knocked down and space reconfigured. What I remember and miss are the smaller cells built for particular activities: the tiny kitchen in Grampy's house where we fried donuts and baked pies, and the blue hand pump on the side porch that squeaked as we worked it up and down to fill the tub for play while the grown-ups talked, and the tiny alcove upstairs where Midge slept when she was a midget. The way people live—what they do in their houses and in their communities—has everything to do with configuration and relationship. Undifferentiated open space seems to be the latest fashion, but in every creation myth I know, worlds are made through separation and differentiation. At Grandmother's, in the big bedroom with twin beds for Midge and Ruthellen (where Katie and I slept when we visited), the twin lift-top desks in the deep bay window are gone. I used to sit there, dreamily staring at Uncle Harry's sawmill, while trying to write school compositions. I distinctly remember one about the migrating whistler swans we'd seen on Batsto Lake, after crawling through melting snow to get close. On August vacations, I'd hear the whippoorwill and other summer night sounds coming through the window, where darkness was a lush violet while thousands of fireflies flashed green-yellow. When I was bored with my book or couldn't think of what to

Author's sister, Jennifer Kietzman, in the Wescoat barn, 1974.

write, I'd lift the desk lid to examine jars of dried up nail polish and bottles of "Evening in Paris," evidence that my mother was the popular and pursued young woman of her stories.

On this trip home, Mom told, as she always did, what I have come to think of as her hero stories, but, this time I listened to the emotional subtext more than surface details because I wanted to understand more deeply how people lived in these places and how it felt to have left them. From the houses, we drove down Pleasant Mills Road toward Batsto and beyond, to the bend in the Mullica River. Mom pulls the car off the road in the place where we used to swim as children. My sister gets out of the car to take pictures, and Mom speaks wistfully of Paul LoSasso, proposing to her years ago "right here." He looked "like Paul Newman" and was her first love. His family lived down the road, and Mom picked strawberries and peaches in the fields behind their house, but they were Italians. "Grandmother made me give the ring back. Yankees down here didn't like the Italians." Mom's was not the only exogamous romance my relatives broke up. When her sister, Ruthellen, eloped with another Italian boy, my mother had to get a different boyfriend—Eddie Marinelli—who happened to be a cop, to "stop them at the Delaware Memorial Bridge." But Yankees weren't the only ones against mixed marriage. From different relatives, I heard the same story of the boy's Italian mother in a long black dress and gloves coming to my grandmother's house, speaking in Italian and with gestures, interpreted to mean that she would cut him off completely if he married Ruthellen. My grandmother is reported to have said how much she loathed hearing "that Dago talk" in her house. Two marriages and probably countless friendships were disrupted by family prejudice that even I had absorbed in childhood from my "ornery" Uncle Philip, who had a derogative for every group that posed a threat to Yankee agricultural dominance.[32] "Going in the houses made me sad," my mother confesses, and I tell her that I felt the same sadness. I get out of the car to put my feet in the Mullica and try to remember those days when, forced to dig potatoes in the hot sun, there was no time to go to Brigantine and Pop would run us up the road for a dip in water that made our bodies look orange. My own pleasure was hard to get hold of, and, instead, I cried for my mother's loss.

"Midge, I can still see you driving that Caterpillar tractor down Pleasant Mills Road," says her old friend Calvin, during our visit. We stop at Calvin's on the way to surveying the different blueberry fields: "there was the twenty-six-acre patch, the ten-acre patch, a field at Weekstown, and a place they called the back meadow." As we drove out Richards' Avenue toward Totem Village,

she remembered how she "drove Calvin crazy" on this very road: "I'd go very fast, and then Bud would yell, 'Stop!' and I'd hit the brakes or 'Turn!' and I'd throw the steering wheel and Calvin would go flying. He was testing my reflexes." As we turn off the paved road onto sand, it is blueberries as far as the eye can see. A white shed in the distance is, Mom thinks, the same packing house where she worked. Involved in telling us all the details, looking across the fields and seeing something invisible to me, she doesn't see the telephone pole. We back into it and the rear window shatters. We get out to inspect the damage and see that glass crystals have fallen all over the beach chairs and luggage. "Boy, I hit that with a good clunk. But, it'll be okay," Mom reassures my daughter. "Look at the blueberries," she moves toward a bush that is loaded with bright fruit (blue with a frosty tinge in the sun). She pops a few into her mouth and urges Katya to do the same. Later the same evening, while drinking beer by the pool at our hotel, Mom admits that she wanted to see the ten-acre field, where we had the accident, because that was where Grampy died. "It was the last field he planted. He wanted to give it to me." He died hoeing his field at night.

The feeling of the day's journey was elegiac: cemetery to long-lost homes to the bend in the Mullica that marked a romance interrupted by fear of immigrants to the field where Grampy died. From thinking hard about these places came my theory about the way Mom's displacement and homesickness motivated her composition of a Nesco mythology filled with unforgettable people—eccentrics, drunks, and farmer heroes. Displacement may also account for her obsessive collecting of coin silver, tin cans, railroad lanterns, brass candlesticks, memorabilia from the '39 World's Fair, and a crank butter churn. My sisters and I used to joke that Mom's house was like an archeological dig. But maybe the hoarding was her attempt at homemaking, recreating the feeling of Nesco, where history was close to the surface and the tools of domestic industry were all around.[33]

Although her displacement was hard on her kids—"Glens Falls was just a place to live"—it also involved us in a multi-generational project of sensing the importance of a place. In that way, I am a bit like Margaret Mead whose mother moved to Hammonton in 1901 to study Italian immigrants. Margaret spent summers of her early childhood living on a farm and picking blackberries, and she returned as an adult to continue her mother's work in a master's thesis of her own titled, "Intelligence Tests of Italian and American Children."[34]

The summer I was ten years old, I convinced my sister Katie, who was a year younger, that we should go to Nesco and pack blueberries. We survived just two weeks of getting up at dawn and packing berries until well after dark, when the fluorescent lights had to be turned on in the barn. We longed for our friends, to swim, and have fun like other kids our age, like we usually did when we stayed across the road at grandmother's. Ruth and Philip's house was dark, and they were strange. I recall one afternoon resting on a bed upstairs: they lay on either side of Katie and me and held hands across our bodies. They were a childless couple. When my mother tells the story of that summer, she tells it as a joke or an illustration of the point that kids today don't know how to work. For a long time, I accepted her interpretation, but now I see that it is wrong. My fieldwork was just different from hers. From an early age, I think I was trying to imagine the Nesco way of life. By volunteering to work for Ruth and Philip, I was trying to live out the experiences of my mother's stories. I was seeking a role in a communal world of work, and I looked forward to staying with my grandmother, whom I loved. Instead, we had to stay across the road in Grampy's house, which was dark and spooky with a weird aunt and uncle who wanted pretend kids. Mom worked with Elmira and other neighbor women, and because of their playful competition, I could see how their work was fun. Katie and I worked alone. It was all wrong.

But I was lucky to visit Nesco five times a year when there was still some farming going on that helped me imagine my mother's different way of life. Even though there were only a handful of family members left on Pleasant Mills Road, we had Batsto, where we knew every nook and cranny of the village.[35] Every time we visited, we made our rounds that began by checking out the skeleton of an ore boat, excavated from the bottom of Batsto Lake in 1957, and the pile of bog ore next to it. We'd feed the horses, look in the barns, and run down to see what the bunnies were up to, hopeful that we could snag peacock feathers from the bird pens. We watched blacksmiths working, listened to the sawmill cutting logs, and learned how the gristmill turned wheat into flour. We spent a lot of time along the lake shore,

looking for pieces of slag—the residue of ironmaking days. Sometimes we'd ride a stagecoach through the village, past the lines of workers' cottages, and, curiously, we never went into the mansion. All of it was very real because we had a relative living in the oldest cottage of all. Olive Wescoat moved into the Spy House after Uncle Harry's death and paid no rent, since she demonstrated quilting to visitors who toured the village in the summer. Aunt Olly's friend lived across the lake, and she became our very dear friend—Annie Carter, the Batsto naturalist, who ran what we called "The Nature House" or "Nature Museum." Annie had a dog, Lady, a possum, and a canoe. We studied the stuffed animals in the cases, told her about the birds and insects we had found, and I read all the quotes from nature writers that she'd tacked into the cedar walls of the house. Words that interpreted, inspired, helped me understand all the reasons why the Pine Barrens were so very special.

My siblings and I made our own nature house in the woods behind grandmother's. We had a wishing well in the crotch of a three-trunked tree. We carried water from the house, sloshing out of buckets down pant legs, out to the woods to fill it so that we could make wishes about the Jersey Devil. There was old farm equipment, which we turned into an exhibit, and we played around and inside the rusted bodies of abandoned Packards. Grandfather had told us that the depression running along the back edge of our "museum" was an old stagecoach line. Each plant, wreck, mark in the landscape had meaning. Looking back on this serious play, I like to think of it as my first attempt at place-making and an early sign that I am Grampy's great-granddaughter.

Children in Nesco were taught in the communal structure of the one-room schoolhouse. My grandmother, Lillian (who really belongs in my pantheon of family heroes), went to Normal School in Glassboro and taught at Weekstown before and, unconventionally, throughout her life as a married mother.[36] In addition to helping one another learn, the twelve students in my mother's class were responsible for menu planning,

Philip Wescoat Jr., Timmy, and Midge, circa 1955.

feeding the coal-burning stove, and getting water from the manual pump behind the school. My mother has a scrapbook from the federal "Schools at War" program that documents the children's efforts, during World War II, to collect scrap metal and sell war bonds and stamps to contribute to the purchase of a bomber that they planned to name "The Spirit of Atlantic County, N. J." Learning school subjects went hand-in-hand with learning to play responsible roles in a community and learning to be active citizens. "Every single effort performed by the children of America," wrote her eighth-grade classmate, Edward Hagaman, "will help in winning the war."

It is generally known that Thomas Jefferson glorified farmers, believing that an agrarian way of life trained up autonomous individuals, each capable of making up his own mind and carrying his own responsibility.[37] While I agree to an extent, the wisdom of Nesco suggests that farmer-heroes grow up in communities and their inventions and industries tend to create the structures for spin-off communities. In my sense of the agglomerate, communities on the edge of the Pine Barrens that embody early capitalism (The Forks), early industry (Batsto and Nesco), and experimental agriculture (Nesco), these places can restore the American revolutionary idea of republican freedom—not a negative or libertarian freedom from constraint or freedom to do whatever one wants.[38] The freedom that communities like Batsto and Nesco educate us for is a freedom to be our individual selves within a communal structure, and that structure is a necessary support and spur to individual creative or entrepreneurial activity. It doesn't surprise me that Hammonton was the place where Emily Fogg Mead did the anthropological fieldwork with the Italian immigrant community that inspired her daughter, Margaret. Nor am I surprised that Kellyanne Conway, former blueberry queen and, like my mother, champion blueberry packer, ran the successful campaign of President Donald Trump and continues to play an important political role as a top advisor. And I am not surprised that her secret service code name is "Blueberry."

If we cannot bring back the one-room schoolhouse or communities like Nesco and Batsto, it is vital that Americans cultivate a strong connection to, at least, one place. I learned about philosopher Josiah Royce's notion of "higher provincialism" from Cornelius Weygandt (1871–1957), professor of literature at Penn, localist, and lover of Jersey. Higher provincialism involves the faith that Americans could best discover what it meant to be an American in service to the social order in its local context; it is basically the same ethos that Jersey settlements have been fostering since colonial times.[39]

Although imagination and spirituality can be devalued in the American narrative that stresses success, mobility, and individualism, I have felt the need to make the trip back to Nesco throughout my life. My contribution to the historical

Weekstown school children conducting a scrap drive: Bud, second from left, and Midge on far right, 1942; Wartime poster drawn by Weekstown pupil, Edward Hagaman.

community is, I hope, to have imagined and understood the lasting value of life as it was lived there. Nesco and settlements like it, though no longer centers of invention and activity, may, by working on our imaginations, inspire us to "Save, Serve, and Conserve" (as my mother's classmate Edward Hagaman put it) communal structures. The archetypal American narrative pushes us from home to search for the new life, the good life, where we can be "ourselves," provided we find "ourselves."

Revisiting Nesco reminds me that human beings are filled with modes of caring that they may have hidden from themselves. Perhaps, then, the more important project is not to decide what to care about after a far and wide search, but to discover, by digging into our native places, what it is about which one already cares. At 86, my mother is still wistful at the turn in the river where, pressed by her Yankee family, she gave Paul LoSasso back his ring. Aunt Ruthellen told me just this summer that "Gran" (Catherine Wescoat Southard), on her deathbed, made a point to apologize for the family's meddling in my mother's romance. Perhaps she wished that they had allowed an Italian to join the family. Perhaps that would have been a way for Nesco to thrive going forward. Perhaps. But if Midge married Paul, then

I would not be here to imagine and celebrate the spirit of Nesco. Wisdom sits in places, but it takes people to work the soil, and that work is necessarily inter-generational because it is physical *and* metaphysical: planting, hoeing, harvesting, packing, remembering, and storytelling. We are still making Nesco, and Nesco is still making us.

ACKNOWLEDGMENTS

I am grateful to Ruthellen Jasper for generously sharing family documents and photos, along with her genealogical knowledge. Bud Walker, his wife Anna, and daughter Cathy Anne arranged a Wescoat pow-wow at the Mullica in the Pines Historical Society museum in Nesco, where it was my good fortune to reconnect with relatives and hear a lot of new family stories. Thanks to Martha and Dave Ware for letting me get a look at William Wescoat's glass medal and to my "piney" cousin, Thomas G. Southard, who carries forward the knowledge of the land in his work with wild plants. Albertine Senske, the archivist at Whitesbog Preservation Trust, provided important information, and my husband, Paul Gifford, the curiosity and encouragement to dig into my own past. The essay is dedicated to my first and best storyteller, Catherine Alice (Midge) Walker Kietzman.

ABOUT THE AUTHOR

Mary Jo Kietzman, Ph.D. teaches humanities courses at The University of Michigan-Flint. She has lived and taught in Ankara, Turkey, and also received a Fulbright grant that took her to Semey, Kazakhstan. She is the author of two books: *The Biblical Covenant in Shakespeare* (forthcoming) and a biography of the early-modern criminal, Mary Carleton. She has published numerous articles on a wide range of English Renaissance authors and subjects, on Lady Mary Wortley Montagu's *Turkish Embassy Letters*, and on Orhan Pamuk's novel, *Snow*. She has also published essays on her work with Kazakhstani students to write and perform an adaptation of *Romeo and Juliet* and with students in Flint to "reassemble" *King Lear*.

ENDNOTES

1 Ronald Reagan visited Hammonton when campaigning for the presidency in the early 1980s and, in a stump speech, referred to the town as the Blueberry Capitol. The town's Chamber of Commerce adopted the slogan officially in 1983.

2 Peter O. Wacker, "New Jersey's Cultural Resources: A.D. 1660–1810," *New Jersey's Archeological Resources from the Paleo-Indian Period to the Present: A Review of Research Problems and Survey Priorities*, ed. Olga Chester (Trenton: Office of Cultural and Environmental Services, Department of Environmental Protection, 1982), 199–219. PDF file at http://www.nj.gov/dep/hpo/1identify/pg_199_NJCulturalResourc1660_1810Wacker.pdf.

3 Arthur D. Pierce, *Iron in the Pines: The Story of New Jersey's*

Midge and Philip Jr. on tractor, circa 1938.

Ghost Towns and Bog Iron (New Brunswick, NJ: Rutgers University Press, 1957), 182. For more details concerning the Elijah Clark plantation, see Matthew G. Hatvany, "*Kate Aylesford*: Modernity and Place in New Jersey's Pine Barrens," *SoJourn* 1, no. 2 (Winter 2016/17): 7–17.

4   Arthur D. Pierce, *Iron in the Pines*, 118–19.

5   Evidence in my own family history that Batsto was producing munitions is found in Stephen Ford's pension application, which states that at the time of the Revolution he was working at Batsto Furnace making cannonballs and guns.

6   John Bezis-Selfa, *Forging America: Ironworkers, Adventurers, and the Industrious Revolution* (Ithaca, NY: Cornell University Press, 2004), 220–21.

7   Charles S. Boyer, *Early Forges and Furnaces in New Jersey* (Philadelphia: University of Pennsylvania Press, 1931), 187. Arthur D. Pierce, *Iron in the Pines*, 144. There is evidence to suggest, however, that indentured servants from Ireland were used at Batsto.

8   Keith H. Basso, *Wisdom Sits in Places: Landscape and Language Among the Western Apache* (Albuquerque: University of New Mexico Press, 1996), 7.

9   J. D. Vance, *Hillbilly Elegy: A Memoir of a Family and Culture in Crisis* (New York: Harper Collins, 2016).

10 Between 1952 and 1960, my mother taught a combined class of grades three and four at Elwood.

11 Robert Bellah notes that the price of concentrating so heavily on the realm of worldly practical achievement in the American narrative was "a thinning out of other dimensions of human experience" like the communal, the imaginative, and the spiritual. Robert Bellah, *The Broken Covenant: American Civil Religion in Time of Trial* (New York: The Seabury Press, 1975), 73.

12 The craftsman's task—and I think this extends to the craft of farming—is "to cultivate in himself the skill for discerning the meanings [and possibilities] that are already there." See Hubert Dreyfus and Sean Dorrance Kelly, *All Things Shining: Reading the Western Classics to Find Meaning in a Secular Age* (New York: Free Press, 2011), 209.

13 Cousin Tom Southard gave me this memory.

14 Walter Ong, *Orality and Literacy: Technologizing the Word* (London: Methuen, 1982), 42–44.

15 My relatives shared the saying that "the aristocrats were in Nesco and the white trash in Batsto," and it is unclear whether this describes accurately or inverts a class distinction.

16 The maternal line in my mother's family conforms to the pattern Janet Nolan identifies. Because Irish servants, who, by and large, emigrated alone, valued teaching, their American-born daughters went to normal school and became teachers. By the first decade of the twentieth century, these women had become one of the largest ethnic groups among public elementary school teachers. See Janet Nolan, *Servants of the Poor: Teachers and Mobility in Ireland and Irish America* (Notre Dame, IN: Notre Dame University Press, 2004), 2–3.

17 As reported by Mike DiMeo Jr., who runs a Pick-Your-Own farm on Pleasant Mills Road, "I didn't want the open fields with dust blowing across but wanted to get back to the way blueberries were originally grown on the edges of woods." His ancestors came to Hammonton from the Aeolian Islands off Sicily when a volcano erupted, probably Mt. Vesuvius, in 1906.

18 *South Jersey Republican* (Hammonton, NJ), August 19, 1905, 1.

19 Philip Gorski, *American Covenant: A History of Civil Religion From the Puritans to the Present* (Princeton, NJ: Princeton University Press, 2017), 31.

20 Juneanne Wescoat Glick, *Waistcote, Westcoatt, Westcote, Westcot, Wescoat, Westcott, Wescott, Wescote, Westcoat, Wasgatt, Wesket, Yegeut, Wisgitt, Etc.* (Clayton, NJ: the author, 1991), 367, 421.

21 Westcoat genealogy, 434, 449.

22 Arthur Pierce, *Iron in the Pines*, 185.

23 Advertisement, *New-Jersey Gazette* (Trenton, NJ), December 18, 1782, 3.

24 Wescoat genealogy, 449.

25 The American Institute of the City of New York was a civic organization that existed from ca. 1838–ca. 1930. The institute was an association of inventors. It organized fairs, exhibitions, lectures, and radio broadcasts to inform the public about new technologies. Medals were issued in gold, silver, and bronze for agricultural and manufactured goods.

26 Wescoat genealogy, 698–701. William Wescoat. Account Books. MC 366. Special Collections and Archives, Rutgers University Libraries.

27 *South Jersey Republican* (Hammonton, NJ), June 14, 1913, 1.

28 All would-be blueberry farmers in this early period would have had to purchase plants from J. J. White, Inc.

29 True-Blue Cooperative, Minutes of Members Meeting, Feb. 8, 1930, Archives, Whitesbog Preservation Trust.

30 Wallace S. Moreland, "Taming the Wild Blueberry," *New Jersey Agriculture* 13 (October 1931): 10–11.

31 Cornelius Weygandt, *Down Jersey: Folks and Their Jobs, Pine Barrens, Salt Marsh and Sea Islands* (New York: D. Appleton-Century Company, 1940), 58.

32 "Ornery" is Tom Southard's word for Philip, who was a complicated man. Spoiled, lazy, obese, he must have been a disappointment to Philip Sr. (Grampy), but Philip had a sweetness to him. I remember him getting so emotional when Midge and family left that he could barely manage to see us off.

33 Each of my mother's siblings has, it seems to me, been driven to remember Nesco. Ruthellen, displaced in Miami, Florida, wrote a family genealogy in the 1970s and ran an antiques business, and Bud, who stayed near Nesco, is one of the founders of the Mullica in the Pines Historical Society, housed in the Hilda Frame school, on Pleasant Mills Road.

34 Cited in Patricia Chappine and Mark Demitroff, "Where Blackberries Grew: Margaret Mead in Hammonton," *SoJourn* 1, no. 2 (Winter 2016/17): 37–43, 40. Emily Fogg Mead's fieldwork was published in a report titled *The Italian on the Land* (1907), submitted to the U.S. Depart-

ment of Labor. For Emily Mead, Hammonton represented a unique assimilation (which my family stories call into question), but this Jersey settlement was also a place of archetypal immigrant accomplishment, which fits my thesis that these settlements near the Pine Barrens offered opportunities for industriousness.

35 The State of New Jersey purchased Wharton's property in the late 1950s and made Batsto a historic village. My mother was one of the first tour guides.

36 Single female teachers were the norm in one-room schoolhouses, and fewer than ten percent were educated beyond high school. Jonathan Zimmerman, *Small Wonder: The Little Red Schoolhouse in History and Memory* (New Haven, CT: Yale University Press, 2009), 29.

37 Jefferson expressed the idea that the number of "husbandmen" determined the health of the body politic in *Notes on the State of Virginia* (1781). Cited in Robert Bellah, *The Broken Covenant*, 117.

38 Settlements like Nesco ballast an American culture that William Williams describes as endlessly repeating its

founding act—rejecting the past for an unrealized and indefinable future. See William H. A. Williams, "Immigration as a Pattern in American Culture," *Immigration Reader: America in a Multidisciplinary Perspective*, ed. David Jacobson (Oxford: Blackwell, 1998), 19–28, 24.

39 "Cornelius Weygandt," Department of English, University of Pennsylvania. https://www.english.upenn.edu/people/cornelius-weygandt. The website notes that "his exposure to the Irish literary influenced his writing with something he called higher provincialism. ["Higher provincialism" was actually Josiah Royce's ideal.] Weygandt's application of higher provincialism developed in him what his colleagues called 'an intense curiosity about our own colonial cultures—their homes, their food, their folkways and arts, and their speech.' He wrote extensively about his own life experiences, particularly the cultural influences from America's past that existed in his life." See Cornelius Weygandt, *Down Jersey*.

Looking due east along Main Street, Batsto, from the western end of the worker village. A man named Will mailed the postcard at Batsto on March 21 1907, and dispatched it "with love" to Mrs. Grace Gridley, Norton Hill, Greenville, Greene County, New York.

Le Balloonist

Hal Taylor

If a survey were conducted (and it could be done by some professional group with a hip contemporary name like, let's say . . . PollCat) comparing those who approve of suburban sprawl, and those who do not, you would undoubtedly find a great number of history fans among the disapprovers. I am one of them, obviously.

I do like the convenience of shopping centers and the like, but there's a terrible price to be paid for easy consumption. Whatever existed before WalMart or Target is gone forever. Most often in the suburbs, farms and woodlands were the predecessors. But occasionally something of truly important historic value is at risk, and, once in a while, some civic-minded people with a reverence for the past will bring forth a motion that a piece of property ought to be saved, and we wind up with a piece of history preserved, no matter how pathetic or disappointing the result is.

Such is the case in the middle of Deptford, New Jersey, in the midst of the aforementioned suburban sprawl. While surely this is not a place where a mighty army was defeated, or where a magnificent temple once stood, it commemorates one of the great events in our country's history. This was where one of man's oldest dreams actually came to fruition—flying, the first time it ever occurred in North America.

In order to pay respects to this event, one has to navigate roadways insufficient to handle the traffic, through a retail jungle, and into the enormous parking lot of a brand-spanking new Walmart Supercenter. Drive past the front entrance and continue around to the back of the store, near the loading docks and recycling bins. Here you will find a low masonry wall that separates Walmart land from the easement of Big Timber Creek. A small parking lot is conveniently provided, and behind that wall is a concrete pathway leading down to a clearing. There you will find a very old and massive oak tree, with a commemorative plaque in front of it. The plaque announces it as "THE CLEMENT OAK," which the Gloucester County Historical Society dedicated during the 300th anniversary of the state of New Jersey in 1964. One can only assume that the tree must have stood on the property of the Clement family, early land owners in the area. There is also Clements Bridge Road nearby that traverses Clements Bridge, a crossing steeped in history. During the Revolutionary War, Hessian troops accessed the span traveling to and from the battle of Fort Mercer in 1777.

In front of that plaque is another smaller one, which reads:

> This Plaque Rededicates the Landing Site of Jean-Pierre Blanchard's Ascension from Philadelphia, on This the 200th Anniversary of "The First Air Voyage in America" Presented on January 9th, 1993 By Favia 200 Inc. & the Township of Depford, NJ.

So what we have is a historic tree and event, neatly combined in one convenient location, much like the one-stop shopping that surrounds it. Obviously, we cannot preserve every scrap of history; there'd be nowhere for the living to exist. But, as innocuous and inconspicuous as this little homage is, at least the attempt was made.

Deptford, one of the original townships in Gloucester County, dating to 1695, was on the outskirts of Woodbury. On the morning of January 9, in that year, a local farmer looked up through the misty sky to see a spherical-shaped object silently descending into a nearby field. It was a large balloon. A man, accompanied by a small, black dog, emerged from it, saw the farmer, and then started speaking to him in an incomprehensible language. Not knowing the man's motives, the farmer stood ready to retreat, should the man show hostile intentions. Much to the farmer's surprise, the newly arrived stranger held aloft a bottle of wine, gesturing for the farmer to come share a drink. The farmer advanced slowly. The stranger was still speaking in an unknown tongue as he brandished some sheets of paper. The farmer cautiously shared the wine and looked at the paper. Since he was illiterate, like many of his day, it was of no use to him. The pilot of the balloon was now faced with a man who could not understand his language, which was French, and couldn't read his document, which was in English.

Another farmer carrying an ancient firearm soon joined the two men. This man could read a little and recognized the name "Washington" on the aeronaut's papers. This seemed to ease the situation a good deal, and the confusion lowered further when more literate people arrived later. Approval was unanimous, and soon, the flying Frenchman, his balloon, and his dog were loaded onto a wagon, transported to Cooper's Ferry on the banks of the Delaware River, and returned to the origin of their flight—the Walnut Street Jail in Philadelphia.

The man whose balloon had just been rescued was Jean-Pierre Blanchard (1753–1809), and it was not the first time he had crossed a major body of water in a balloon.[1] Blanchard had been fascinated with flying machines, and experimented with them numerous times in his native town of Normandy. His repertoire primarily consisted of machines with wings, which included a flying tricycle.[2]

In addition to Blanchard, there were other native Frenchmen such as Joseph Montgolfier and his brother Étienne who were interested in creating and flying prototypes of large paper balloons filled with heated air. Their first successful flight occurred in 1783 using a balloon that was thirty foot high, with a circumference of 110 feet, and required eight men to keep it earthbound. When released, it rose to the dizzying height of 6,000 feet, and remained aloft for ten minutes.[3] It was the

Jean-Pierre Blanchard. *All artwork by Hal Taylor.*

Montgolfier brothers who also engineered the first manned flight in the same year, which carried two aeronauts over the city of Paris for 27 minutes. This event made instant heroes of the first men to fly.[4]

When Blanchard learned of the success of balloons as aerial conveyances, he abandoned his flying tricycle and began making his own balloons. He did not abandon his earlier concept of wings altogether, but continued to experiment with them, and also came up with an early type of hand-cranked propeller which was known as a moulinet. He realized that, to this point, a balloon was at the mercy of the wind, with no way to control its direction.

Blanchard's early trials were successful, but also expensive. In the fall of 1784, he moved his operations to London in hopes of finding private backing. It was here that Blanchard began to cement a reputation not only as a fearless pioneer of flight, but also as a pompously self-absorbed man, perhaps due to his lack of physical stature.[5]

Blanchard dined with the Duchess of Devonshire, and met with the cream of the English scientific world, including Sir Joseph Banks, long time president of the Royal Society. Blanchard's most important acquaintance was Dr. John Jeffries, a native of Boston. Jeffries was a major advocate of balloon flight relative to studying the upper atmosphere and the weather. He agreed to back Blanchard and also to accompany him with an assortment of the latest in scientific instruments on a series of flights sanctioned by the Royal Society.[6]

Now they were ready for the biggest challenge to date: crossing La Manche—the English Channel, for which Jeffries coughed up the breathtaking sum of £700. Preparations were made and a date was set for the historic flight, when Blanchard, true to his nature, suddenly announced that it would be a solo flight—the glory would be his alone.

Jeffries was greatly distressed by the news, and the two men argued violently until the Governor of Dover Castle intervened on behalf of Jeffries. The wily Blanchard continued to try to capture all the attention for himself by devising the outlandish scheme of secretly wearing a lead-weighted belt under his coat and then arguing that the balloon would simply be too heavy to carry both men aloft. Jeffries was not fooled.

Blanchard then refused to carry any of Jeffries' scientific equipment on board, but gave in to Jeffries' demand for a barometer and a mariner's compass. They also carried cork jackets—in case they had to ditch, thirty pounds of sand ballast, a package of letters and publicity pamphlets, and one bottle of brandy. Both men were impeccably dressed for the occasion: Jeffries in a beaver flying hat and expensive chamois gloves, and Blanchard in silks and the latest finery that the French fashion world

Blanchard's descent into Gloucester County.

had to offer. Finally, at one o'clock p.m. on January 7, 1785, the two men ascended from the cliffs of Dover to attempt the first crossing of a major body of water by balloon.[7]

The ascent went smoothly enough; initially, the balloon sailed along in an easterly direction toward Calais, but about two-thirds of the way across the channel, the airship began to lose altitude. It was clear they would not be able to rise above the cliffs of the Pas de Calais, let alone the sea, so they began to jettison anything that was not of absolute necessity. When that failed, they stripped off their outer garments, leaving both men about to enter France, or the ocean, in their underwear. Still, the balloon continued to descend. There was only one desperate option left, the undignified act of evacuating themselves.[8] That did the trick.

Approaching the coast, the updrafts helped to lift the men over the shoreline. They bounced along the treetops of the French countryside until Jeffries was able to grab enough branches to gradually slow them down. They climbed down from the trees where the balloon had come to roost, gradually deflating, and shivered from the cold until a crowd of spectators who had been following the flight on horseback soon arrived to carry them to Calais. Somehow, the bottle of brandy survived the flight, as well as the parcel of letters, which became effectively, the first airmail delivery. Among the letters was one from Benjamin Franklin's son, William, addressed to his son, Temple.

Later, the two were celebrated royally in Paris, where Jeffries spent several evenings with Benjamin Franklin, pondering the future of flight . . . and the beauty of French women.[9] Blanchard received a royal pension and became the toast of Paris, celebrated as one of the first aeronauts. Trying to capitalize on his notoriety, he opened a "Balloon Academy" in England, but it eventually failed, and he returned to France. Blanchard then set out on an ambitious tour to promote the new science of ballooning, which was now termed aerostation. From 1785 to 1788, he exhibited his aeronautical prowess to the delight of

audiences in Germany, Holland, Belgium, Switzerland, Poland, and Czechoslovakia, before turning his attention to America.[10]

On September 30, 1792, Blanchard departed from London on board the CERES, and landed in Philadelphia on December 9. He lived there for the next year, raising money and making preparations for the first successful aerostat flight in the New World. He was able to strike a deal with the city fathers for the use of the Walnut Street Jail, which would provide a controlled environment for the safety of the balloon, and, an exclusive venue for a paying audience of up to 4,500. He reasoned that if he could sell 500 front row tickets at $5 apiece, and another 1,000 at $2, he would be handsomely reimbursed for his efforts. However, Philadelphians, being a tight-fisted bunch, decided the view would be just as good from outside the prison yard. As a result, Blanchard only managed a gate of a little over $600 total, which was not nearly enough to cover the cost of scientific instruments and other apparatus used for the launch, or the massive balloon itself, the circumference of which measured a hefty 100 feet.[11]

The event was well publicized, and as a result, there were huge crowds on hand. They were kept in anticipation by the firing of two artillery pieces every quarter hour, as well as a brass band playing their most rousing tunes.[12] Since Philadelphia was the capital of the U.S. at this time, it can be fairly certain that Vice President John Adams and future presidents James Monroe and James Madison were on hand, as well as the then-Secretary of State Thomas Jefferson. Also in attendance was John de Ternant, the minister plenipotentiary of France.

The ascension was scheduled for 10 a.m., and at 9:45, a carriage pulled up bearing the country's first chief executive, George Washington. Washington exchanged pleasantries with Blanchard, speaking to the diminutive Frenchman in his native tongue about the historic importance of the occasion. Just as he was to depart,

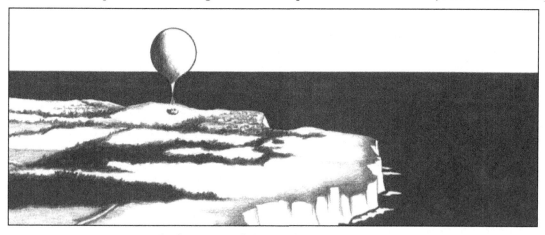

The first manned flight over the English Channel.

Washington uttered a closing statement to Blanchard: "One more thing, Monsieur. In order to guarantee your safe passage upon completion of your voyage, it would please me if you would take this letter with you." With that, he presented Blanchard with a hand written passport addressed to "all citizens of the United States, and others, that . . . they oppose no hindrance . . . to the said Mr. Blanchard" and assist him in his efforts to "advance an art, in order to make it useful to mankind in general." This is the document he would later waive in the face of the very baffled South Jersey farmer.[13]

Blanchard thanked the President and stepped into the large, bathtub shaped wicker basket strung underneath the balloon. Someone presented him with a small, black dog, which he awkwardly accepted, placing it on the floor of the gondola and prepared for the ascent. The artillery fired a final deafening round, and Blanchard threw out some ballast. The silk balloon, which was described as being "yellowish in color, highly varnished, and covered with a strong net work," rose about fifteen inches above the ground, at which point Blanchard gave the order to his two assistants, Peter Legaux and a Dr. Nassy, to release the guy wires.

As the enormous aerostat rose gently, the crowd gazed intently upward. Blanchard waved his hat and a two-sided flag identifying the U.S. on one side and France on the other.

The balloon rose steadily until a mild breeze began to carry it eastward, and, in a matter of moments, it was over the Delaware River. Blanchard later wrote: "This river appeared to me like a ribband of the breadth of four inches." The balloon, at this point, was drifting at a steady altitude of 5,800 feet, and Blanchard took the opportunity to perform a number of atmospheric experiments. Dr. Benjamin Rush, a pioneer in psychiatry and signer of the Declaration of Independence, had asked Blanchard to time his pulse when he reached his maximum altitude, and Blanchard obliged, observing 92 beats per minute—8 beats more than when he was on the ground. He then filled six bottles with "that atmospherical air wherein I was floating" at the request of famed physician Dr. Caspar Wistar. Blanchard then turned his attention to the weather, observing a thick fog toward the south, and mist rising from the east, the direction in which he was heading. Ever the Frenchman, Blanchard paused to refresh himself with a morsel of biscuit and a glass of wine.

Sighting what he believed to be the Atlantic Ocean far in the distance, he decided it was time to get ready to descend. Forty-six minutes after drifting without incident from Philadelphia to an open field near Woodbury, New Jersey, Jean Pierre Blanchard became the first human to fly in the New World.[14]

Blanchard stayed in Philadelphia in an attempt to raise money for a second flight by opening an "aerostatical laboratory," in which he charged a nominal fee to see his now-famous balloon and a variety of his own wacky mechanical whimsies. When little interest and money was generated, he moved on to Charleston, South Carolina, in 1795, where his fortunes did not improve. Boston and New York proved to be no more lucrative, and Blanchard eventually returned to his native country of France in May of 1797. Finally, he was able to resume balloon flights, making thirteen more until what would have been his sixtieth flight, when he suffered a heart attack. He died a short time later on March 7, 1809. He was just 56.

Marie-Madeleine-Sophie Arrant, Blanchard's widow, carried on her husband's legacy by becoming an aeronaut herself. Tragically, she became the first woman to die in an aerial accident when her balloon caught fire during a flight in 1819, and she fell to her death.

So ends the story of the first manned flight in the New World, commemorated almost anonymously on the outskirts of a department store parking lot in Deptford.

ABOUT THE AUTHOR

Throughout a long and varied career Hal Taylor has been a musician, typographer, type designer, college professor, illustrator, and lately, an author. His first book, *The Illustrated Delaware River: The History of a Great American River*, was released in late 2015. A second book, *Before Penn: An Illustrated History of the Delaware River Colonies*, is completed and due to be released shortly. A third volume, *The Book of Wedges*, from which this article is an excerpt, is a work in progress. Hal makes his home in historic New Jersey. You can view his work at www.haltaylorillustration.com.

ENDNOTES

1 C. V. Glines, "First in America's Skies," originally published in *Aviation History* (September 1996); republished 6/12/2006, http://www.historynet.com/jean-pierre-blanchard-made-first-us-aerial-voyage-in-1793.htm.
2 Richard Holmes, *The Age of Wonder* (New York: Pantheon, 2008).
3 Ibid., 129–52.
4 Ibid.
5 Ibid.
6 Ibid.
7 Ibid.
8 Ibid.
9 Ibid.
10 Alan Drattell and Jeanne O'Neill, *Journey to Deptford* (Deptford, NJ: Township of Deptford, 1976), 15.
11 Ibid., 20.
12 "First in America's Skies."
13 Ibid.
14 Ibid.

Purple Pitcher Plant blossoms,
(*Sarracenia purpurea*),
photographed June 5, 1971.
Courtesy of Ted Gordon.

Pyxie-moss (*Pyxidanthera
barbulata*), photographed
April 18, 1980. *Courtesy of Ted
Gordon.*

Elizabeth C. White's Garden

Albertine Senske

A chapter extracted from the forthcoming SJCHC publication, *With Eager Hands: The Life of Elizabeth Coleman White.*

Your garden—it refreshes me just to think of it and the blissful restfulness of it all! Elizabeth Kite[1]

Elizabeth C. White. *Courtesy of the Whitesbog Preservation Trust.*

Today, Elizabeth Coleman White is best known for her work cultivating the first commercial blueberries in collaboration with Frederick V. Coville. But White was a master agriculturalist with an interest in a wide range of plants that thrived in the Pine Barrens. Her garden in Whitesbog, New Jersey, was known throughout the region. Many came to visit and enjoy its beauty. An article published in the January 30, 1938, edition of *The Trenton Sunday Times* announced a series of fundraising garden tours with Miss White's garden as one of the venues. The proceeds benefited St. Mary's Hall, a private Episcopal girls school in Burlington.[2]

What made the garden so special? Elizabeth tells us herself. "The charm of every garden depends largely on the happy relationship of its open spaces to trees, bushes and flower borders."[3] And of course, on the unique selection of trees, bushes and flowers. For her garden at Suningive, her home at Whitesbog, Elizabeth primarily chose species indigenous to the small area of the globe she called home. Why did she love the entire community of native plants? The answer is simple: her Grandfather James Fenwick and father Joseph J. White. Elizabeth must have been very young, probably under five, when she received her first lesson from a doting grandfather.

The great pear tree was full of bloom and bees and spicy fragrance that sunny afternoon years ago when Grandfather Fenwick called his little granddaughter to see what he had brought her from "the bog."

There . . . in grandfather's hand was a bunch of the long-stemmed dark red flowers of the Pitcher Plant (*Sarracenia purpurea*).

These flowers came from "the bog" where Grandfather Fenwick had started in 1857 the culture of cranberries. Many were the treasures that came to that little granddaughter from "the bog": great mats of Pixie-moss (*Pyxidanthera barbulata*) thickly dotted with pink buds which opened into starry, white flowers (see p. 28); spicy red Tea Berries (*Gaultheria procumbens*), a delight to the eye and so good to eat; a tiny turtle perhaps or a stem of Tiger Lilies (*Lilium superbum*).[4]

When the child was ten she lost her grandfather and her father Joseph J. White took charge. . . . It was his daughter's delight to share his plans and to associate with the lovely wild bog plants.[5]

A particular favorite of Elizabeth and a rare plant of the bogs was the Pine Barren Gentian (*Gentiana autumnalis*). She writes:

> The day I first saw it is engraved in my memory as clearly as the day I first saw the Pitcher Plant flowers.... In the morning the bogs were too wet to pick and I was free for a few hours. So father and I, in the buggy behind plump, brown Daisy, started off to see how picking progressed with our neighbors a few miles away.
>
> The winding, sandy road wandered through a stretch of low ground where water stood in the ruts. On the two parallel ridges between the wheel tracks and that worn by horses' hoofs were little hedges of all the native plants.... Like the whole country, these little hedges were glorious with the maroon, crimson, green and gold which autumn brings to the bog country of the Jersey Pines.... Suddenly amid the green of dwarf Laurel (*Kalmia angustifolia*)[6] and Sand Myrtle (*Leiophyllum buxifolium*) and the crimson of the Huckleberry (*Gaylussacia baccata*)[7] I spied a spot of bright blue. It was a gentian. We found five or six of them that morning.... The wide, open flowers were two inches and more in diameter, with five petals spreading out from the morning-glory-like throat, and a fringed septum joining the pointed petals for about a third of their length.[8]

The Pine Barren Gentian (*Gentiana autumnalis*) in October. *Courtesy of Ted Gordon.*

Elizabeth was in her 50s before her famous garden became a reality. We have no record of such a garden at the family home at New Lisbon, where she lived from 1881–1924, but that does not preclude its existence or suggest that a hiatus occurred in her interest in native plants. One has only to peruse her early photographs to see the hold these wonders of nature had on her. There are several pictures of Pitcher Plants, Grandfather Fenwick's gift; it also appears *Monotropa uniflora*, commonly known in the area as Indian Pipes, held a fascination for her.

Oral tradition has long held that Elizabeth White used the bequest left to her in her mother's will in 1923 as seed money to build a home at Whitesbog that she named Suningive. While the inheritance funds may have enabled actual construction to begin, a recent foray into the company minutes shows that plans for a Whitesbog home began before her mother's death which occurred November 1, 1922. At the February 6, 1922, board meeting, a motion was introduced to build a house for Elizabeth at Whitesbog. The motion carried with the following stipulations: the building would serve first

and foremost as her home. At the same time, it would provide Joseph J. White, Inc. with a company dispensary, a venue to entertain company guests, and a site for clerical work and other purposes. In compensation for company use, J. J. White, Inc. would contribute $5,000 toward construction, as well as pay for insurance, repairs and taxes. Elizabeth would be responsible for the remaining construction cost, funded with a 6 percent interest loan, and for ongoing costs to provide light, heat, provisions and "help."

Elizabeth was not the first White daughter to consider a home at Whitesbog. Frank and Anne (White) Chambers cleared land for a home shortly after Frank began to work at the farm in 1911. They quickly abandoned plans due to Anne's health and the need for closer proximity to medical assistance.

Emlen and Mary (White) Darlington actually built a house at Whitesbog in 1914 and lived there for a year before returning to Fenwick Manor. Elizabeth

Elizabeth C. White's house, Suningive, 1928. *Courtesy of Whitesbog Preservation Trust.*

The East Garden at Suningive. *Courtesy of Whitesbog Preservation Trust.*

was the only one to remain permanently in her own house at Whitesbog. The placement of the house had significance for her. Rimmed by pines, swamp cedars,[9] Red Maples, Gray Birches, Sour-Gums, and Swamp Magnolias, the ground on which Suningive was built had, for ten years, been one of the original blueberry test fields. A row of bushes, discarded for their fruit, but of lovely form and foliage, determined the exact location of the house which also overlooked one of Grandfather Fenwick's first cranberry bogs.[10] Around the area were also Swamp Azalea (*Rhododendron viscosum*), Aronia, or Red Chokeberry (*Aronia arbutifolia*), and Inkberry (*Ilex glabra*), all tangled with Greenbriar. As Miss White noted, "Good material this, but the effect was battered, bleak, unorganized."[11]

The main garden was not Elizabeth's first project. Grading was needed close to Suningive. Soil excavated from the blueberry patch left a hollow that she filled with water from a nearby irrigation ditch. With the water came lily seeds. By the second summer, there were green lily pads, and a year later glorious flowers. White was enamored of the beauty that surrounded her and she had the soul of a poet when describing it. In regard to the need for a yearly thinning out of the water lilies, she provides as a rationale, "to insure open water to mirror sunsets, the moon, and stars."[12]

Once the pond area itself was finished, Elizabeth began her primary landscaping project. As a foundation, she planted Mountain-laurel (*Kalmia latifolia*) and Inkberry (*Ilex glabra*), balancing their deep evergreen coloring with the lighter leafage of Red Chokeberry and Blueberry (*Vaccinium*). Like the blueberry bushes that formed the hedge around her home, the Grover #2 did not make the grade as a fruit producer, but it surpassed every other variety in the magnificence of its deep crimson coloring in autumn. Red Chokeberry offered two seasons of beauty. In spring, it put out flowers like tiny apple blossoms, while in fall, bright red berries graced the arched stems.

Elizabeth compared the work of a gardener to that of a sculptor, who shapes a lump of clay by adding some material here, removing some there, until a pleasing form emerges. Mats of Bearberry, already covering several areas closer to the house, were left in place for both beauty and usefulness.

> Its small, upright branches are covered with little leathery leaves, dark green in summer, red-brown in winter; in spring they are decked with tiny, inverted, pearly, pink-tipped urns, and later red berries. The mats of Bearberry (*Arctostaphylos uva-ursi*) nurse many other plants of briefer beauty, such as the fall-flowering goldenrods, purple and white asters, and purple wands of Liatris which open their flowers from the top down.[13]

Red Chokeberry (*Aronia arbutifolia*): (left) in May, (right) in October. *Courtesy of Ted Gordon.*

Elizabeth C. White's Garden

Liatris may sound unfamiliar and exotic, but most of us know it, thanks to the cut-flower industry. The long, purple spikes of *Liatris* often grace formal floral arrangements, or may be included in a supermarket bouquet. This plant belongs to the aster family. Common names include Grass-leaf Blazing Star or Grass-leaf Gayfeather. Witmer Stone called it Hairy Button Snakeroot (*Lacinaria graminifolia* var. *pilosa*), while other botanists referred to it as *Liatris graminifolia*. Today, it is known as *Liatris pilosa*. When the stalk begins to flower, the first buds appear at the top of the spike, which allows the top of the stalk to be cut off while the lower portion continues to bloom.

It would not be a Pine Barrens garden without moisture-loving plants, nor would it be Elizabeth White's garden without Pitcher Plants, Grandfather Fenwick's first gift from the bogs. She called sphagnum moss the "best nurse" for these additions to the landscape.

> This was planted at the margins of the pool, sometimes in mats but often in little tufts four or five inches apart which soon covered the ground. Here are the Pitcher-plants. Some of the leaves, with their beautiful red veining, hold more than half a glass of rain water. In early summer, on stalks 18 inches high, these plants dangle flowers with big, floppy maroon petals. They drop soon after bees have brought pollen to the stigmas at the tips of the five ribs of a curious, inverted, central umbrella. The stems hold high the umbrella and glossy sepals until late fall, when the ripe seeds scatter.[14]

The Rose Pogonia (*Pogonia ophioglossoides*), photographed June 26, 1977. *Courtesy of Ted Gordon.*

Pine Barrens orchids, another favorite, were abundant around the pool. Elizabeth calls it a troop of Rose Pogonias (*Pogonia ophioglossoides*) and notes the single, pale pink, delicately scented flower that topped each eight-inch stalk. This beauty was not isolated to the New Jersey bog lands. Robert Frost celebrated it in his first volume of poetry, *A Boy's Will*, published in 1915.

Rose Pogonias

A saturated meadow,
Sun-shaped and jewel-small,
A circle scarcely wider
Than the trees around were tall;
Where winds were quite excluded,
And the air was stifling sweet
With the breath of many flowers,—
A temple of the heat.

There we bowed us in the burning,
As the sun's right worship is,
To pick where none could miss them
A thousand orchises;
For though the grass was scattered,
Yet every second spear
Seemed tipped with wings of color,
That tinged the atmosphere.

We raised a simple prayer
Before we left the spot,
That in the general mowing
That place might be forgot;
Or if not all so favoured,
Obtain such grace of hours,
That none should mow the grass there
While so confused with flowers.[15]

One commentator calls Frost's offering a magical image, the description of a fairyland. White was an avid reader. Did she know of this poem? Did she read it?

There are no volumes of Frost in what has been passed on as Elizabeth White's library, but the reverence for nature exhibited in Frost's work is a reflection of that found in Elizabeth's own life and writings.

Two other Pine Barrens orchids found a home in the garden, Grass-pink (*Calopogon tuberosus*) and the White Fringed Orchid (*Platanthera blephariglottis*). These three graced the landscape from May into July. Although different species, each was covered with red hairs, tipped with a sticky dew-like droplet to catch and, then, digest small insects. A collection of Venus Flytrap from North Carolina was a later addition to the garden. It is a bit surprising to hear the kind, big-hearted Elizabeth admit, "What fun to feed the leaves flies or tiny grasshoppers and see them quickly snap shut!"[16]

Elizabeth chose her plants with careful thought so that she would have blooms throughout the seasons. Summer must have provided a riot of colors for her enjoyment. Orange Milkwort (*Polygala lutea*) mingled with Gold-crest (*Lophiola aurea*), mats of Pyxie-moss, Pine Barren Gentian and Climbing-fern (*Lygodium*

Grass-pink (*Calopogon tuberosus*) in July. *Courtesy of Ted Gordon.*

palmatum). Pyxie-moss and Sand-myrtle (*Leiophyllum buxifolium*) seem to have captured her descriptive imagination.

> The structure of this tiny shrub [Sand-myrtle] has, in miniature, all the picturesque rugged dignity of old rhododendrons. The small evergreen leaves have the same leathery quality. Starry white flowers smother the plants in May, but before the flowers open each little bush has its own individual bud color. Some are crimson, some pink, and others greenish white.[17]

Perhaps the most loveable of all the Pine Barren plants is the Pyxie (*Pyxidanthera barbulata*),[18] frequently called Pyxie-moss or even Flowering Moss [photo, p. 28]. It is really a woody shrub with evergreen leaves, but, unless struggling in the shade of larger shrubs, it grows no more than half an inch high. Its prostrate branches spread out on the surface of the ground. When young the plants are green stars flat on

White Fringed Orchid (*Platanthera blephariglottis*) in late July. *Courtesy of Ted Gordon.*

the earth with five or more slender branches one to two inches long. As the plant grows older it forms a mat, for all the world like a patch of starry moss . . . Early in the spring each green star of the mossy surface develops in its center a pearly pink bud. These open into flat, five-peaked, white flowers, a quarter of an inch in diameter, each just touching its neighbors, . . . When in full bloom and viewed from some distance Pyxie looks like a dropped white handkerchief.[19]

Elizabeth loved all her Pine Barrens plants, but she also invited guests into her garden, plants from other localities that could thrive in Pine Barrens landscapes. Among the introductions were Scotch Heather, Carolina Rhododendron and the Venus Flytrap previously mentioned. She knew she had created something special; Suningive and the surrounding garden made a unified whole. The only thing missing was a lawn.

How lovely is a good lawn! But so difficult to maintain on the sand surrounding Suningive. The cranberry bog would serve as the lawn. It had been started by my grandfather, had furnished

Both photos Sand-myrtle (*Leiophyllum buxifolium*) in May. *Courtesy of Ted Gordon.*

the means for Suningive, and inspiration for its garden. For 100 acres from the windows it stretches to the distant, dark, encircling rim of pines. Its velvety surface, green in summer, gradually turns to deep maroon by the middle of October. In December the bogs are flooded and, for garden purposes, lawn becomes lake—deep blue beneath clear skies; flashing with diamonds on sunny days; dark and glowering, with white caps racing before an easterly storm wind; smooth, still, and shining when Jack Frost lays his quieting hand upon it.[20]

Elizabeth wanted others to appreciate and love the beauty of the bog-lands as she did. As her grandfather and father had tutored her, she was willing to spend time introducing others to her magnificent world, if only they were receptive. Elizabeth Kite was one of her pupils. Kite describes one of their sessions:

> Our objective that morning was "Buffin's Meadow," a great wilderness of untamed bog-land, and our car drew up when we touched its outmost rim.

(Above, June 22; below, early July) Threadleaf Sundew (*Drosera filiformis*). *Courtesy of Ted Gordon.*

Elizabeth C. White's Garden

Stilled by an inner awe, as well as by the voice of my friend, I sank on a mossy bank, hands clasped in ecstasy, for before me, on a slight elevation, glittering in the sun's bright rays, was what seemed an innumerable company of tiny fairy folk suddenly stopped in a merry round danced to faint bog-land music. . . . What were they, this fairy folk, so dainty and so gay in the morning sun? Indeed, they were old friends, but never before had I seen them so numerous or so dazzling beautiful. For the instant, I seemed transported to a world as remote from the great city I had left as though I had landed upon some distant planet. In reality, these tiny folk were superb specimens of *Drosera filiformis*, or Sundew.[21]

While it was a joy to create new enthusiasts by personal, one-on-one instruction, it was a limited approach. Elizabeth seized opportunities as they presented themselves. In a letter to Chester M. Chaney of the American Cranberry Exchange, she expressed regret for having missed the August 1932 Annual Convention of the American Cranberry Growers Association. She explained her absence:

> The Flower Show in Atlantic City offered a rare opportunity to introduce to nurserymen a couple of plants for which we were desirous of securing a wholesale outlet and when we were urged to put on a Wild Garden we accepted the chance. We believe we made good, but only time will tell.[22]

The Atlantic City show was a three-pronged success. Elizabeth was able to educate nurserymen in Pine Barren plants and promote sales; a large audience had the pleasure of actually seeing the beauty of a garden

Elizabeth C. White in her garden at Suningive. *Courtesy of Whitesbog Preservation Trust.*

like Elizabeth's; and Elizabeth and her nurseryman Tom Windon came home to Whitesbog with a medal.

Emerging technology offered Elizabeth another alternative. In the late 1870s, Heinrich Hertz discovered radio waves. Inventors vied to develop practical applications and, by 1910, these various wireless systems had come known as "radio." Bamberger Broadcasting Service established WOR radio in 1922. Louis Bamberger owned a chain of department stores in New Jersey. He thought his employees could sell radios much more easily if the store were to operate its own radio studio, which he located on the sixth floor of the store's Newark headquarters. One of the more popular programs airing over WOR was the Radio Garden Club. Elizabeth White appeared on this show twice that can be substantiated. On June 6, 1937, she presented a recap of her blueberry experiences, and, in 1941, she spoke about her garden of Pine Barren plants. The transcript from this latter broadcast provided most of the plant descriptions identified above as filling her garden. Others come from articles written for the *Bulletin of the American Rock Garden Society* and *Wise-Acres*, a publication of the Pennsylvania School of Horticulture for Women.

Acknowledgement

Ted Gordon, Pine Barrens historian, botanist, and authority on Whitesbog history, has helped in numerous ways in the development of this chapter from the forthcoming biography of Elizabeth C. White, *With Eager Hands*. In addition to providing twelve floral images, Ted has updated both the scientific and common names in this article. I thank him for so willingly sharing his knowledge.

About the Author

Albertine Senske is the archivist of the Whitesbog Preservation Trust where she has been a volunteer for the past twenty years. A former educator, Senske joined the Education Committee, serving as a tour guide and lecturer. In conjunction with her archival duties she continues her research into the White and Fenwick families as well as the history of both cranberry and blueberry industries. Current efforts of the Archives Committee include making portions of the Whitesbog Archives available online.

Endnotes

1 Letter from Elizabeth S. Kite to Elizabeth C. White, May 3, 1931, Whitesbog Preservation Trust Archives.

2 "Mrs. B. B. Locke Named Chairman of Garden Days," *Trenton Sunday Times*, January 30, 1938, part two, 3.

3 Elizabeth C. White, "My Garden of Pine Barren Plants," MSS for Program of the Radio Garden Club of New Jersey, Station WOR, March 24, 1941, 2, Whitesbog Preservation Trust Archives.

4 The flower that White calls Tiger Lily is presently known as Turk's-cap Lily.

5 Elizabeth C. White, "Some Bog Plants of the Jersey Pines," *Wise-Acres*, publication of the Pennsylvania School of Horticulture for Women (Ambler, PA, 1929): 70. White used Witmer Stone's botanical plant names in *Plants of Southern New Jersey* (1911); where needed these have been updated to modern taxonomic identifications as well as common names in accordance with Alan Weakley's *Flora of the Southern and Mid-Atlantic States* (2015).

6 Dwarf Laurel is today known as Sheep Laurel (*Kalmia angustifolia*).

7 The Huckleberry that White refers to, *Gaylussacia baccata*, is the Black Huckleberry.

8 White, "Some Bog Plants of the Jersey Pines," 71.

9 Swamp Cedars are today known as Atlantic White Cedar (*Chamaecyparis thyoides*).

10 The bushes were Haines #9, an early variety of blueberry cultivated by White and Coville.

11 White, "My Garden of Pine Barren Plants," 1.

12 Ibid., 2.

13 Ibid., 2–3.

14 Ibid., 3.

15 Robert Frost, *A Boy's Will* (New York: Henry Holt and Company, 1915), 25–26.

16 White, "My Garden of Pine Barrens Plants," 3–4.

17 Ibid., 4–5.

18 Elizabeth preferred the spelling Pixie, rather than the more common Pyxie.

19 Elizabeth C. White, "Plants of the New Jersey Pine Barrens," *Bulletin of the American Rock Garden Society* 1 no. 2 (May–June 1943): 54.

20 White, "My Garden of Pine Barrens Plants," 2. This bog, affectionately known as "Old Bog," is no longer being cultivated, but the same panorama can be seen from the windows of the upper floors of Suningive replacing Fenwick's bog with those in actual production today. They just aren't close enough to be considered Suningive's lawn.

21 This is the Threadleaf Sundew. Elizabeth Kite, "Sights and Sounds of Bogland," 2, Whitesbog Preservation Trust Archives.

22 Letter from Elizabeth C. White to Chester M. Chaney, September 13, 1932, Whitesbog Preservation Trust Archives.

Pocahontas on the Delaware:
The Intersection of History and Legend in the Historiography of New Jersey

John W. Lawrence

On January 5, 1633, a simple transaction occurred on the banks of the Delaware River near the mouth of Big and Little Timber Creeks. Goods were exchanged for information in a transaction between a Lenni-Lenape woman and the Dutch patroon, David Pieterszen de Vries (Figure 1). This was de Vries' second voyage to the Delaware River, which served the dual purpose of privateering and whaling. In 1633, he was 40 years old and an experienced and well-respected navigator who had already sailed five of the world's seven seas. Despite his experience, however, on that early January day, de Vries was in trouble, and he knew it.

One month earlier, the Dutch contingent of 34, sailing in two ships, had landed at Swanendael, a palisaded settlement de Vries had established in 1631, near what is today Lewes, Delaware (Fig. 2). Captain de Vries and crew arrived at Swanendael on December 6, 1632, only to find the bones of virtually all its inhabitants and their livestock scattered throughout the settlement and surrounding fields.[1] Several days were required to entice the local Nanticoke to parley and for de Vries to establish what had transpired.[2] Not surprisingly,

Figure 1. 1655 Portrait of David Pieterszen de Vries. *From de Vries, Korte Historial, 1655.*

conflict based on cultural misunderstandings had erupted between the Nanticoke and Dutch settlers, probably not long after the settlement was established. It is not, however, a typical story of European hubris and intransigence leading to conflict and death.

As the assembled Nanticoke revealed to de Vries, the Dutch had erected a post in the settlement onto which they had affixed a tin plaque painted with the Dutch coat of arms, by which they established possession of the land. According to the Nanticoke, "one of their chiefs"[3] had removed the plaque to make a pipe, which had much angered the Dutch. This act in itself, however, did not lead directly to inter-ethnic conflict and eventual loss of the colony. Apparently, in an attempt to appease the Dutch, the Nanticoke killed the sachem who had removed the plaque. They only informed the settlers of the event *ex post facto* when the natives delivered the chief's severed head to the Hollanders. The Nanticoke then explained to de Vries that it was "friends of the murdered chief [who] incited their friends"[4] to wreak vengeance on the Dutch for the death of their sachem. The natives successfully ambushed the settlement and avenged the death.

David de Vries did not provide any details of the number or composition of the Native American groups involved in the Swanendael incident, but the reference to Nanticoke "chiefs" killing one of their own to appease strangers suggests that more than one band of Nanticoke were present. If so, the entire incident may reflect inter-band conflict and competition for access to valuable European trade goods the Dutch likely possessed. In calculating his response to this turn of events, de Vries determined that revenge (his word) was not an option, "as they [the Nanticoke] dwelt in no fixed place."[5] This telling observation by de Vries—that there was no Nanticoke village near Swanendael—reinforces the notion that one or more bands were temporarily camped nearby in order to trade. Re-establishing warm relations with the Nanticoke offered de Vries the best alternative, and he possessed sufficient experience to know that to cement peace required tangible evidence of good will. Accordingly, he "gave them some presents of duffels [cloth used in trade], bullets, hatchets, and various Nuremburg trinkets."[6] Although he does not specifically say as much, de Vries was enough of a tactician to know that to continue north up the Delaware River he needed to secure his rear, which required peace with the Nanticoke to the south.

While certainly a smart move, the gifts given to the Nanticoke left de Vries ill-equipped for further trading with the Native Americans he would encounter upstream. As the primary economic objective of the voyage was whaling and privateering (in which it had not been successful)—it was not a trading mission—the vessel held only a small stock of trade goods. The serious problem de Vries and crew faced, as they sailed upriver during the dead of winter, was the fact that the expedition was running low on food. After dealing with the Nanticoke they now had little to trade to obtain much-needed provisions.

On January 1, 1633, Captain de Vries and seven of his crew left Swanendael in the yacht SQUIRREL and by the evening of January 2, arrived at Reed Island, a

journey of about 50 miles upriver. By January 4, they arrived "within cannon shot" of Red Hook (present-day National Park in Red Bank, Gloucester County), probably anchoring off the mouth of Woodbury Creek. The next day, they sailed another three or four miles north to their destination: Fort Nassau, a fortified trading post the Dutch established in 1626. Although the precise location of this fort has been lost to time, the best available evidence places it on the eastern shore of the Delaware somewhere near the mouth of Little and Big Timber Creeks.[7] At the time of de Vries' 1633 visit, the Dutch had abandoned the fort, but the Lenni-Lenape occupied its palisaded walls. Some of these Lenni-Lenape belonged to the Sankitans band from the north and others of the Mante band from the Red Hook area to the south. In de Vries' own words:

Figure 2. Detail of Visscher and Schenk's 1690s Map, showing locations of Swanendael and Ft. Nassau. *Novi Belgii Novæque Angliæ, 1690s.*

> Some Indians had assembled there to barter furs, but I desired to trade for their Turkish beans,[8] because we had no goods to exchange for peltries, and our stores had been given away at Swanendael for the purpose of making the peace, so that there were not more than two pieces of cloth left of our goods, and two kettles, for which we wanted corn.[9]

After informing the Lenni-Lenape that he was not prepared to trade for their furs, but instead sought to trade for food, de Vries noticed a change in their attitude. The Lenni-Lenape requested that he bring his ship closer to shore to trade and it was at this point that a Lenni-Lenape woman of the Sankitans band warned de Vries that the Lenni-Lenape actually planned to attack them. It was here that our transaction occurred. In de Vries' own terse journal entry:

> When we told her that if she would relate to us everything in regard to the attack, we would give her a cloth garment, as we did. She confessed to

us that they had killed some Englishmen, who had gone into Count Ernest's river[10] in a sloop.[11]

As events transpired, no conflict ensued at Fort Nassau, and it is unknowable whether any attack was in fact ever intended, despite the warning. On January 8, members of the nearby Mante band did board the SQUIRREL to trade, but de Vries became nervous and they were shortly after ordered off at gunpoint. However, over the next three days de Vries successfully traded with increasing numbers of Lenni-Lenape who arrived at Fort Nassau to trade. He appears to have traded with members of up to nine different Lenape bands. Captain de Vries obtained his much-needed maize and—despite his protestations of insufficient trade goods—beaver pelts, in exchange for iron axes, adzes and knives. After further adventures on the river, David Pietersen de Vries and crew sailed out of the Delaware Bay on March 20, 1633, never to return.

A Legend Born

David Pieterszen de Vries' *Korte Historiael ende Journaels Aenteyckeninge van Verscheyden Voyagiens in de Vier Deelen des Wereldts-Ronde, als Europa, Africa, Asia, ende Amerika gedaen* (*Short Historical and Journal Notes of Various Voyages in the Four Quarters of the Globe, Namely, Europe, Africa, Asia, and America*) was first published in Alkmaar, the Netherlands, in 1655 (Fig. 3). As the title suggests, de Vries based his work on a personal journal he maintained during his voyages. By the early nineteenth century, the work had grown exceedingly rare and no verbatim translation in English appeared in print until 1841.[12] The 1841 translation by Dr. Gerard Troost, *Extracts from the Voyage of De Vries*, is exactly that: selected extracts. Troost, a Dutch medical doctor, mineralogist, naturalist, and first President of the Philadelphia Academy of Natural Sciences, translated only certain passages from selected dates in de Vries' journal. His publication lacks significant passages from the journal.

Prior to the Troost translation, the only access in English to de Vries' account of New Netherlands was through the publication of Joseph Moulton's 1827 *History of New York*[13] and Thomas Gordon's 1834 *History of New Jersey*.[14] Moulton credited Troost with providing him with an as-yet unpublished English translation of de Vries' journal.[15] With it, Moulton provided a fairly complete account of de Vries' experiences on the Delaware River. Gordon based his narrative on the account found in Moulton's publication. It was not until 1857 that a complete English translation of de Vries' journal covering his 1632/33 journey up the Delaware River was published. Henry C. Murphy produced the full translation for the New York Historical Society.[16]

In the de Vries journal, as translated by Troost and Murphy, as well as in the Moulton and Gordon narratives, the exchange between the unnamed Sankitans woman and de Vries occupies no more than four or five lines.[17] Moulton was the first, however, to insert a new element to the story—one that came to increasingly overshadow if not dominate de Vries' own words in histories of New Jersey written over the ensuing one hundred years. Moulton likened the unnamed Sankitans woman to Pocahontas and pointed out that de Vries' experience was but only one instance of native women assisting Europeans.[18] Gordon echoed this observation when he stated that it was: "the interposition of an Indian woman, so often recorded in favour of the whites" that saved de Vries from destruction.[19] With those few words, "so often recorded in favour of the whites," Gordon subtly introduced a story within the story, as Moulton had before him, that de Vries' experience was not a singular event but part of a repetitive pattern in history. Neither Moulton nor Gordon identified this inferred pattern of history beyond the fact that it involved Native American women saving European men. Subsequent writers on the history of New Jersey would clarify the point.

Figure 3. Title page to de Vries' *Korte Historiael*.

David de Vries' brief encounter with a Sankitans woman underwent significant transformation and was given dramatic life in a story written by a Mrs. M. A. Ford entitled "Mahala: A Legend of New Jersey." Published in the May 1843 edition of *Miss Leslie's Magazine*, Mrs. Ford referred to her work as a "sketch," not a history, written to "cherish a grateful memory of a gentle daughter of their [Sankitans] tribe." The "legend" in the story's title is a literary conceit only and the ensuing tale is an elaborate confabulation written fully within the Romantic literary tradition of the time. In the story, Ford gave the unnamed Sankitans woman the name Mahala and she was transformed into the daughter of one Sankitans chief and wife to another.

Ford's "sketch," which incorporates elements of de Vries' experiences at both Swanendael and Fort Nassau, is simple and brief. The principal driver of the story's plot involves a significant modification of historical events as de Vries had recounted them. In "Mahala," it is the Dutch who execute the Nanticoke chief responsible for removing the coat of arms at Swanendael, not the Nanticoke themselves. This plot device provides a rational, if morally misguided, motive—revenge—for the Indians' planned attack on de Vries and crew at Fort Nassau.[20] Returning to the story, the beautiful and virtuous Mahala overhears the plan and escapes the village, taking advantage of the cover of darkness and the inebriated condition of the other Indians who had partaken of "the white man's cup." In another inversion of de Vries' history, Mahala is already dressed in European cloth when she goes to warn de Vries, rather than the Dutchman giving the cloth in reciprocity for her information, as had actually happened. This seemingly insignificant detail becomes a key element in the Romantic import of the story. Ford describes her:

> Mahala now made an effort to overcome her timid nature and advanced nearer to the table [where de Vries sat]. The lights revealed more fully the striking beauty of her countenance and figure. Across one shoulder was fastened a piece of scarlet cloth, confined at the opposite side by a band of beads of the same colour, and gathered in folds at the waist, descending nearly to the feet, leaving free the beautifully moulded arms.

Mahala's price for informing the Dutch of the planned attack no longer consisted of mere material goods, which, according to Ford's story, she already possessed. Mahala sought something much grander, much nobler. Mahala extracted from de Vries the promise that he would not wage war on her people if she informed him of the planned attack. Hers was a heroic and selfless action, performed with no thought of personal gain. Ford also painted de Vries as a romantic figure ("His rich light hair fell in curls over his white forehead and the glow on his cheek contrasted with the bright blue of the eyes. . . ."), who was smitten by Mahala's beauty, grace, and innate goodness. He did offer her material riches (she refused) and offered to take her back with him to Holland, to which she replied: "Mahala will not leave her forest home. Her child sleeps in the wigwam of its father. She would rather die than part from it." Mahala's intervention saved the Dutch from destruction, and the story ends in protestations of filial love between the two protagonists as the Dutch depart safely downstream. David de Vries declared himself to be "the brother who will always love thee" and Mahala responded that she "will be the white man's sister . . . and if he ever forget mercy for the Indian, let him think of that sister."

The "Mahala" story should be seen as a not atypical example of historical romanticism of the mid-nineteenth century. While the Mahala character is not an example of the Noble Savage, she is certainly a child of nature of the Romantic conception. She exhibits all the superior physical and moral characteristics of womanhood that, in the romanticist's imagination, express themselves in their purest form when untainted with the corrupting influence of civilization and its attendant materialism. Her innate purity, love, and loyalty allow her to act as a disinterested mediator between two worlds and save both from annihilation—immediate in the case of the Dutch expedition and eventual in the case of the Lenni-Lenape.

The parallels are obvious between the "Mahala" and Pocahontas stories, as Joseph Moulton first remarked in 1827. Although little is actually known of Pocahontas's life, the story of her intervention to save Captain John Smith was—and continues to be—reinterpreted in the Romantic tradition through a variety of media (Fig. 4).[21] In poetry, prose, theater, and graphic arts, Pocahontas has been particularly malleable; she has been transformed into an advocate for woman's rights,[22] medicine woman, spy, entrepreneur, and diplomat,[23] and even thanked for her "services rendered to our race and country"[24] (Fig. 5).

Although perhaps the best-known exemplar today, Pocahontas as a literary figure is not the only analog to Mahala. There is, for example, the widely circulated novella *Atala*, which François-René de Chateaubriand published in 1817 (Fig. 6). The alliteration of Atala and Mahala itself suggests a commonality of theme

Figure 4 (above). 1616 Portrait of Pocahontas engraved by the the Dutch and British printmaker and sculptor Simon van de Passe. *Courtesy of the British Museum, London and wikipedia.*

Figure 5 (right). Romanticised 1883 version of Pocahontas. Note the similarity of the image with Atala (on the following page) and the bared arm and shoulder à la Mahala. *From Mary Cowden Clarke,* World Noted Women *(New York: D. Appleton and Company, 1883).*

Figure 6. Title page for François-René, vicomte de Chateaubriand's *Atala. From* Atala, *printed with two other titles:* Indian Cottage *by J. H. B. Saint-Pierre; and* Idyls; *and* First Navigator *by Solomon Gessner (London: Walker and Edwards, 1817).*

and plot that is, in fact, borne out. While significant differences exist between the two literary efforts, both revolve around a heroine, a child of nature, who must mediate between representatives of Native and European cultures. In the case of *Atala*, the heroine sacrifices her life to her sense of honor, thereby elevating her as a tragic, romantic figure. Pocahontas and Atala are just two examples of the widespread use of Native American themes in early-to-mid nineteenth-century romantic literature. Van Wyke Brooks reminds us that by 1830, over 60 plays had been performed in the New York City theater alone treating "with Indian characters and Indian themes."[25] Native Americans indeed proved to be fertile ground for the romantic imagination.

The History of a Legend

Mrs. Ford's romantic "sketch" made an immediate impact on the historiography of New Jersey. Within a year, John Barber and Henry Howe published their first edition of *Historical Collections of the State of New Jersey* (1844), and cited Ford's publication, where they did not cite either Troost's earlier translation or the bona fide historical accounts by Moulton or Gordon. More importantly, Barber and Howe adopted and expanded the message of "Mahala" as first expressed by Moulton and fully integrated into Ford's ersatz legend. In Barber and Howe's own words:

> This incident concurs with a thousand others, to show that kindness is an essential quality of the female heart, whether it beat in the savage or the belle; and the true lover of virtue cannot but regret that the name of De Vries' benefactress, because unknown, must remain forever unhonored and unsung.[26]

Whereas Barber and Howe closely followed de Vries' account of events at Fort Nassau, the historical lesson that they drew from that account—on the role of women and the importance of virtue—was the message that Barber and Howe wanted their readers to understand.

On the heels of Barber and Howe's *Historical Collections*, Isaac Mickle published his *Reminiscences of Old Gloucester* in 1845.[27] Much like Barber and Howe, Mickle directed his readers to the "well written tale" of "Mahala," but he relied substantially on the events at Fort Nassau as de Vries recounted them. Nevertheless, Mickle added a new element to the story, one not seen before, but one that crops up again later in the historiography of New Jersey. In discussing the Native American motive for their planned attack on de Vries, Mickle states that they were "animated by a deadly hate of the ravishers of their wives."[28] Here, Mickle breaks new ground by accusing the Dutch of molesting native women. Mickle provided no source for this accusation, which is not found in any preceding accounts of events, much less in de Vries' journal. The accusation, however, animates the dramatic narrative by providing even deeper motivation for the intended Indian attack. Together with this elaboration, Mickle deepened and expanded the historical lesson of the de Vries experience:

> Thus the wide world over, do we find gentle woman laboring to counteract the cruelties of man—preventing if she may, the blow that impends, or if it must fall, blunting its edge,

and averting its effects, regardless of the risk to herself. This nameless heroine periled her life to save De Vries. . . . Her generous bravery in the cause of mercy does much to alleviate the dark traits in the character of the Indian, and she deserves to be remembered forever, as an ornament to her sex and her race.[29]

Over 30 years later, in its Wednesday, March 1, 1876, edition, the *West Jersey Press* reprinted "Mahala: A Legend of New Jersey" in its entirety. According to the editor of the weekly newspaper, the reprinting was done by anonymous request, but the editor's preface to the reprinted story included the statement that Dutch "outrages" on Nanticoke women contributed to the destruction of Swanendael—a contention entirely missing from the Dutch account and not made until Mickle's 1845 *Reminiscences*. A seemingly random and isolated retelling of the "Mahala" story, this reprinting would influence later histories of Camden and New Jersey.

The tale makes makes its next appearance, without using the name "Mahala," in Frank Stockton's 1896 *Stories of New Jersey*, a collection of isolated events in New Jersey from the time of European discovery to the mid-nineteenth century. In his *Stories*, Stockton is equivocal as to whether they should be taken literally as history; however, putting on a historian's hat, he provides the primary source material that informed each chapter. In the case of de Vries' second visit to the Delaware River, Stockton cites Brodhead's 1871 *History of the State of New York*.[30] Even the title of Stockton's story, "The Story of a Peacemaker: An Indian Woman's Friendly Act" belies the fact that the story relies much more heavily on previously published histories of New Jersey than on Brodhead's history of New York. We know this because at no point did Brodhead mention that it was a *woman* who saved de Vries. Brodhead merely states that "a Sankitan or Stankekan Indian warned the Dutch."[31] Stockton also refers to the Sankitans woman who warned the Dutch as a "wife of one of the Indian chiefs,"[32] which of course was an invention of Ford's "Mahala" story and not found in de Vries' journal nor in Brodhead's work.

While Stockton's "Peacemaker" contains a terse reiteration of events that occurred between 1632 and 1633 at Swanendael and Fort Nassau, it incorporates an expanded presentation of themes introduced earlier by Gordon, Ford, Mickle and others. It was Stockton's contention that Native American women fulfilled an indispensable social function as peace negotiators between warring factions or tribes, where in native

societies male honor would not allow men to treat for peace.[33] Stockton thereby reified into a societal role what had been, to previous authors, just a natural inclination of women. Nevertheless, like previous writers, Stockton also celebrates the traditional "guardian angel," who saved David de Vries and crew, and finishes the story with:

> Whether or not he [de Vries] rewarded the good woman who came to warn him of his danger, is not known; but his account of the affair places her in the position of one worthy of a monument by the women of the State.[34]

Of course, we do know that she was in fact rewarded with cloth duffel, a fact that to Stockton tarnished the heroic dimensions of her act and which he therefore omitted from his tale. The power of the "Mahala" story impacted the imaginations of New Jersey residents in such a way that the New Jersey Society of the Sons and Daughters of the Pilgrims raised a monument to "The Indian Maid" in 1937 (Fig. 7).[35]

Ten years after Stockton published his *Stories*, Howard Cooper published an expanded version of a paper he had delivered ten years earlier, entitled *Historical Sketch of Camden, N.J.*[36] In his history of the city, originally read before the Camden County Historical Society, Cooper includes under the rubric, "aboriginal legend and pioneer romance," a condensed retelling of the "Mahala" story. Cooper acknowledged his sources for the story— Ford's original 1843 publication and the 1876 *West Jersey Press* reprint—but referred to the narrative as "A well told story founded *on this incident* [emphasis added]," leading the unwary reader to view his recap of Ford's roman-

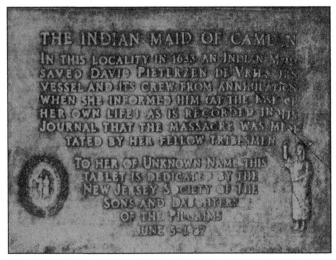

Figure 7. Historical marker in Camden's Farnham Park as seen in the early 1950s.

tic "sketch'" as a historical "incident."[37] Whereas earlier writers had hewed fairly closely to the de Vries account while elaborating on its historical significance, Cooper effectively re-categorized a romantic literary tale into a historical fact. Although Cooper mentions de Vries in his work, he apparently chose not to use his first-hand account, at the time easily available in either the Troost or Murphy translations. Instead, he availed himself of earlier writers who conflated events at Swanendael and Fort Nassau and repeated the undocumented assertion that the Dutch had molested native women at Swanendael.[38] Finally, Cooper decided to repeat the comparison between the "young Indian mother," who bartered with de Vries, and Pocahontas, a comparison not made explicit since 1826, serving to underscore his Romantic reading of the event.[39] It is difficult to understand why Cooper, an avid reader of history, would have chosen to include a reiteration of the "Mahala" tale in his history of Camden, when he was undoubtedly aware of the various translations of de Vries' journal.

MAHALA AND THE INTERSECTION OF MYTH AND HISTORY

Not all nineteenth-century historians who wrote about events on the Delaware River in the early seventeenth century chose to mention David de Vries' encounter with a Sankitans woman. Those that did, despite similarities in their presentations, came from varied backgrounds. Joseph White Moulton (1789–1875) was a New York attorney and historian who also authored a study of chancery law in the state; he is recognized further for basing his historical studies on primary source material.[40] Born in Philadelphia and also an attorney, Thomas F. Gordon (1787–1860) turned towards writing popular histories in the late 1820s.[41] He began with his native Pennsylvania, but turned to broader subjects before publishing his *History of New Jersey* in 1834. For it, the state legislature not only provided financial support, but granted the author access to any records or documents from the state library that he deemed necessary.[42]

Both John Barber (1798–1885) and Henry Howe (1816–1893) were Connecticut Yankees who teamed as business partners to write a series of financially successful state history books, employing a template and methodology Barber used for his first book, *Connecticut Historical Collections* (1836). Barber began his career as an engraver, and his 1836 publication was widely successful for its skillful mixing of local images with historical content, collected from informants as Barber personally crisscrossed the state.[43] Howe, son of a bookseller, became acquainted with Barber's work (and its financial success)

through his father, and proposed to partner with Barber. Together they produced three publications, of which their *Historical Collections of the State of New Jersey* was the second. For their New Jersey volume, the authors described their methodology in the following terms:

> In collecting the materials for this work, we have travelled over the State, conversed with her most intelligent citizens. . . . We have, moreover, solicited written communications from gentlemen in all parts of the state, embodying facts of great value, which could be properly prepared only by those who resided on the spot.[44]

Whereas Barber and Howe would have been considered artisans in American society of the time, Isaac Mickle (1822–1855) was a gentleman. The scion of a wealthy and respected Quaker family from what are now Camden and Gloucester counties, Mickle was one of the "gentlemen" from whom Henry Howe sought information for the *Historical Collections of the State of New Jersey*. At first, Mickle appears to have been much flattered and provided Howe with what he knew about the Camden area; however, he was less happy later about what actually appeared in print.[45] Mickle described Howe as "a true example of the Yankee character—shrewd, quick and observing" and remarked with an air of condescension that: "He travels on foot, carrying his knapsack with him, and a little book in which he dots down all his gleanings."[46] Class differences between the two men aside, this is not the kind of comment one would expect from someone sufficiently experienced with or appreciative of the hard work of "doing" history.

Isaac Mickle was an accomplished dilettante in several fields, of which history was but one. According to his journal entries, his interests ranged from politics, to music, to women, to law, to journalism, to history, more-or-less in that order. He spent a great deal of his time in leisurely pursuits appropriate to the gentry and he had difficulty focusing on his studies for the bar, which he nevertheless passed with plaudits from his examiners in 1844. A birthright Quaker, there is no indication that he was an active member of the Society of Friends. To the contrary, he preferred to listen to and engage with members of all denominations then present in Philadelphia and Camden. An ardent and partisan Democrat, Mickle believed in equality of opportunity for all men, but not in the social equality of all men.

Mickle himself acknowledges that he originally had no intent to write a book on the history of Gloucester County and his diary entries prove that his editor occasionally harried him to maintain the publishing schedule.

It appears Mickle completed some chapters in haste and Mickle's diary contains few entries related to the work of writing his *Reminiscences*. One finds only sporadic references to visits to the Free Library of Philadelphia, or to the Surveyor General's Office in Burlington, or to Woodbury to review documents. He also solicited information from prominent local citizens via correspondence.[47]

As with John Barber and Henry Howe, Francis Richard Stockton (1834–1902) was a professional writer, although history represented but a small part of his oeuvre. Stockton was a popular, best-selling author of the late nineteenth century, best known for children's books and juvenile literature, but who turned towards an adult audience later in his career.[48] Born to a prominent Methodist minister in Philadelphia, Stockton did not advance beyond a secondary school education, but became a tradesman, first as an engraver and later as a journalist. During his career as a journalist, writing for Philadelphia and New York newspapers, he turned to writing literature. An autodidact whose literary output advanced from magazine articles to short stories to novels, Stockton's works were known for their ". . . high moral tone. All his works breathe an especially pure and whole spirit. Whether writing for men and women or for children, he was actuated always by the noblest and loftiest impulses."[49] "His characters are, without exception, moral men and women."[50] Interestingly, for all the popularity of his prodigious output of fiction, Stockton's works of non-fiction have elicited little to no subsequent commentary or review. Nonetheless, the "high moral tone" that he injected into his telling of the "Mahala" story is easily noted.

Like Isaac Mickle, Howard Cooper (1844–1922) was also the scion of a well-established Quaker family in Camden and a prominent citizen of the city. In fact, Howard's mother was a Mickle, but Cooper appears to have been of a very different temperament from Isaac. He attended a Quaker institution (Haverford College) for his Bachelor's and Master's degrees and remained a life-long active member of the Religious Society of Friends. Like Mickle, Cooper also joined the legal profession. After having passed the bar in 1867, he spent a lifetime in private law practice and dedication to the public good, serving as a founding member, or otherwise significantly involved, in innumerable voluntary civic and professional associations in the city and county.[51] According to his daughter, reading local history was only a hobby for Howard Cooper, but he maintained enough interest in the subject to be a founding member of the Camden County Historical Society in 1899 and its President from 1919 to 1922.[52] His written output on the subject is limited to the *Historical Sketches*, based, as we have already mentioned, on a lecture presented to the Historical Society in 1899. According to his daughter, he also "wrote various other slighter papers on local history . . . for presentation at meetings of various sorts."[53]

Despite their varied backgrounds and level of involvement with history as a discipline, the authors who related the "Mahala" story all had one thing in common: to the extent that they revealed their philosophy of history, each author expressed an unfailing dedication to telling the unbiased truth.[54] Truth, however, had more than one dimension in their writing and thinking. The unbiased truth to which our authors explicitly referred involved the search for pure, unvarnished facts. In their eyes, the role of the historian was to remove the passions and biases of their sources that could infect the truth of their historical narratives. As Thomas Gordon explained:

> More particulars of the horrors which attended the revolutionary war . . . might, perhaps, have been added [to Gordon's history], if full reliance were due to the partial newspaper accounts, frequently *written under excitement unfavorable to truth* [emphasis added].[55]

But there was a greater, unspoken Truth in these historical narratives that allows us to understand the persistence of "Mahala" in the historiography of New Jersey. A clue to this thinking can be found in the opening paragraph of Charles Joline's introduction to Howard Cooper's 1909 book:

> If one were to seek the genesis of Camden he would not find it in the visit of the sturdy Dutchman, DeVries, nor of any explorer who followed, nor in the voyages of the those in search of a land where they might increase their worldly possessions, but rather would he find it in souls devoted to the principle, and primed with courage never to yield; in a quiet contest for right and equality, which knew no submission.[56]

Today it is easy to glide over Joline's fanciful rhetoric as belonging to the age of Sunday strolls and the Gibson Girl, but it provides an important clue to our question. What Joline was saying—and what Cooper and his predecessors undoubtedly would have seconded—is that history is not the details of actual historical events ("the visit of the sturdy Dutchman") but the inexorable unfolding of progress toward a better and more just world ("a quiet contest for right and equality"). This is the deeper truth of history; what history instructs us.

David Levin, in his *History as Romantic Art*,[57] describes this understanding of history, and the proper role of the historian during the nineteenth century. For these historians, history as a process was the gradual revelation of unchanging moral laws as established by Providence. The basic assumption was one of continual, if at times faltering, human progress. Levin evokes the metaphor of a spiral to describe the course of this progress; it was not always direct—the spiral could widen and flatten out at times—but it was ever upwards.[58] Although unstated, it was also clear to these historians, and presumably their readers, what was the apex of this spiral: White, Protestant, Western European society, and preferably the variety found in England or New England. The task of the historian, then, was to sift through the facts, "the dross of history,"[59] and reveal the "gold" within—the unfailing moral story of human progress towards a more perfect society.[60] The resulting narratives these historians crafted sought to reveal that segment of the spiral that pertained to the historical event(s) or period then under consideration. The insistence that the facts used in these histories had to be unbiased, objective reality merely cemented the truth of the underlying, upward spiral of progress.

In the hands of our authors, the persistence of the "Mahala" story is an example of the unstated, romanticized truth of history. Mahala is the gold within the dross, the example of moral progress amongst the sordid details of actual events that gives weight, meaning and instruction to History as Progress. The particular moral lesson of Mahala, developed and expanded with the re-telling of the tale, is consistent with the Romantic-era conception of women being, in their essence, different from men. Where men are competitive, inherently amoral, and prone to violence, women are cooperative, nurturing, virtuous, and peace-loving. To maintain their civilizing effect on men, it was appropriate for men and women to hold sway in separate spheres or domains— the public domain being proper for men and the domestic sphere for women.

Joseph Moulton and Thomas F. Gordon just barely expressed this essentialist view of women in the early 1800s—they merely noted that women frequently interposed to assist and aid men—but the view became increasingly elaborate during the ensuing course of the century and beyond in the evolution of the "Mahala" tale. It is also appropriate to note that when discussing the essential quality of women in the context of de Vries' experience, the text in these stories shifts from past to present tense, underlining the timelessness of these qualities and the historical lesson being taught. To Barber and Howe, "kindness *is* an essential quality of the female heart"; to Mickle, "Her generous bravery in the cause of mercy *does* much to alleviate the dark traits in the character of the Indian"; and to Stockton, "the affair *places* her in the position of one worthy of a monument." And, at least to Isaac Mickle, this was no literary trope. His diary entry for May 16, 1841, reads: "This danger [of him falling in with a bad crowd] would be removed by an extension of my female acquaintance—by changing the billiard-room for the drawing room."[61]

By the late nineteenth and into the early twentieth century, the period in which Richard Stockton and Howard Cooper were professionally active, faith in the kind of progress that had animated earlier nineteenth-century thinkers was becoming considerably constrained. For one, belief in the inevitability of human progress began to falter. By the mid-nineteenth century it was difficult for western Europeans to understand why colonized peoples around the world did not readily accept the obvious benefits of Western civilization brought to them by their masters.[62] Doubts then arose as to their innate capacity to do so. By the early twentieth century, this thinking solidified as scientifically-endorsed concepts of race, and racial determinism justified the denial of progress to non-white Americans.[63] Not coincidentally, the role of women in society and the nature of femininity itself was also coming under re-evaluation; consequently, the essentialist view of women's nature and compartmentalized role of women in society that it endorsed came into question.

It is generally recognized that the history of the women's suffrage movement and the broader women's movement is complex and fractious.[64] That said, most historians agree that the call to recognize the independent civil, social, political, and religious rights of women was first enunciated in the United States with the "Declaration of Sentiments" at the 1848 Seneca Falls Convention. Although one element of the women's movement was concerned with the kind of social reforms befitting the nurturing, protective role of women as understood and espoused by the earlier Romantic vision, the means and methods that later nineteenth-century women reformers used to attain their ends did not fit within the prescribed "separate spheres" for men and women. The core of the new philosophy—as boldly stated in the Declaration of Sentiments—was that women had the right and the ability to act in the public sphere to obtain the social and political policies and outcomes they sought. They no longer had to work their influence through their fathers, husbands or sons to effect change, as had been the case when women were confined to their own domestic domain.[65]

Paradoxically, Stockton and Cooper elaborated on the essentialist theme to the "Mahala" story as society's view of womanhood was evolving in a different direction. That evolution remained slow and was certainly not the mainstream social thinking of the period; however, it is worth noting that several of the leading voices in the woman's movement were Quakers with connections to the Delaware Valley. Four of the five organizers of the Seneca Falls Convention were Quaker women.[66] Perhaps the most influential was Lucretia Mott (1793–1880) of the Cheltenham Meeting, but the group also included Lucretia's sister Martha Coffin Wright (1806–1875), educated in Philadelphia, Mary Ann McClintock (c. 1795–1884) of Philadelphia and Jane Clothier Hunt (1812–1889), also born and raised in Philadelphia. Philadelphia-area Quakers, such as Alice Paul (1885–1977) of Mount Laurel, were represented in the next generation of activists in the cause of women's rights. The fact that the Philadelphia Yearly Meeting decided in 1920 to abolish its practice of separate meetings for men's and women's business—a practice held since the seventeenth century—tells us that a degree of consensus had arrived among the area's Quaker community about the equality of men and women.[67]

It is unclear to what extent these intellectual and social currents influenced Frank Stockton. In his "Story of a Peacemaker," the balance sheet between traditional and progressive thinking on the role of women comes out even. On the one hand, Stockton created a concrete social role for women in native society (such as the suffrage movement attempted to do), while simultaneously placing them on a pedestal as essentialist "guardian angels." In contrast, Howard Cooper, as a practicing Friend within the orbit of the Philadelphia Yearly Meeting, could not have been ignorant of progressive thinking on women's issues. It is striking, then, that Cooper not only chose to recount the essentialist moral of the "Mahala" story in his history of Camden, but that he would invest so heavily in it by repeating M. A. Ford's romantic tale. We can only speculate about why he made the decision to copy the story. Freedom of conscience is an enduring quality of Quakerism and Cooper, an influential pillar of Camden society, may simply not have agreed with the more progressive thinking of his religious compatriots. His flourishing legal practice and innumerable philanthropic and organizational activities obviously made him a busy man and it may simply have been easier to copy a ready-made, "well told story" than to sort through and recount the messy details of historical fact.

Faint echoes of "Mahala," and the story's Romantic-era overlay, have continued until the present day.

As mentioned above, in 1937, a historical marker was erected in Farnham Park, Camden, to honor her story. In 1948, an article published by members of the Camden County Historical Society recounted de Vries' experiences, but only mentioned that a Native American woman had alerted him to a possible attack.[68] More recently, a local history published in 2014 refers to a "young Lenni-Lenape mother" who aided de Vries, a statement that again merges elements of "Mahala" with de Vries' original diary account.[69]

POCAHONTAS ON THE DELAWARE AND THE LESSONS OF HISTORY

If the purpose of history is to instruct us—as we are so frequently reminded about what happens to those who forget it—what are we to make of Mahala, or the Pocahontas of the Delaware? Historian Gordon Wood has argued strenuously that we must respect the "pastness of the past," that is, the fact that it is strange and different and needs to be understood on its own terms within its own context and without anachronistically projecting onto it contemporary ideas and perspectives.[70] But even if we avoid the pitfalls of presentism,[71] can we truly write about the past without making it comprehensible in the present? Nineteenth-century historians made David de Vries' experience comprehensible by linking it to common and deeply-held cultural beliefs current at the time about the nature of femininity and the role of women in society. Here, we have described de Vries' experience differently, from the perspective of contemporary, anthropological, and historical understandings of how Native American societies were structured, operated, and interfaced with early European explorers. This contemporary understanding of native societies tends to focus on their internal political dynamics and recognizes the existence of intra-tribal as well as inter-tribal conflict and competition—conflict and competition that Europeans successfully exploited. There is no room for Mahala in this contemporary perspective, but does that make it a more accurate rendering of the past, or merely another version of it?

Historian E. H. Carr[72] reminds us that there can be no historical consciousness without the knowledge that there will be a future different from the present. That, perhaps, is the ultimate lesson that Mahala provides us: that the present conditions our understanding of the past and will continually evolve as the present unfolds into the future. The "facts," as we know them, of the encounter between David Pietersz de Vries and an unnamed Sankitans woman will never change. How we relate to and understand them will certainly change, and appropriately so, as our own society changes and evolves.

ABOUT THE AUTHOR

John Lawrence is a resident of Burlington City and, as Senior Archaeologist, has practiced archaeological and historical investigations across the mid-Atlantic states for a number of consulting firms over the past thirty years. His professional experience has included original research into the history and prehistory of South Jersey, in which he has a particular interest in historic farmsteads and farm life. Mr. Lawrence is a former Commodore of the Red Dragon Canoe Club on the Delaware River, one of the oldest, continuously operating boat clubs in the country.

ENDNOTES

1 News of the massacre had already arrived in the Netherlands before de Vries departed for the New World. Apparently a single survivor of the massacre escaped to New Amsterdam, from which the news travelled back to the Netherlands. E. B. O'Callaghan, *The Documentary History of the State of New York* (Albany: Weed, Parsons & Co., 1850), 30; Charles McKew Parr, *The Voyages of David De Vries: Navigator and Adventurer* (New York: Thomas Y. Crowell Company, 1967), 115.

2 The Nanticoke, like the neighboring Lenni-Lenape, comprised one of many Algonquin-speaking tribes that lined the eastern seaboard from New England to the Carolinas in the early seventeenth century.

3 Henry C. Murphy, "Voyages from Holland to America, A.D. 1632 to 1644," in *Collections of the New York Historical Society*, Second Series, vol. III (New York: D. Appelton and Company, 1857), 23.

4 Ibid.

5 Ibid., 24.

6 Ibid. Nuremburg was a leading manufacturing center of the age and known for producing small trade items that Europeans carried on expeditions around the world. Carl Zehden, *Commercial Geography of the World* (London: Blackie & Sons, 1889), 247.

7 Edward Armstrong, *The History and Location of Fort Nassau upon the Delaware* (Newark: Daily Advertiser Print, 1853). Armstrong hypothesized that the fort was situated on the tongue of land formed at the mouth of the Big and Little Timber Creeks; other evidence suggests that it was located on the high river terrace south of the Big Timber Creek. Others historians have placed it north of Little Timber Creek, in contemporary Gloucester City.

8 A native bean, probably the Kidney bean; "Turkish" was an adjective signifying "foreign" to the Dutch, i.e., not native to the Old World. Edward Eggelston, *The Transit of Civilization from England to America in the Seventeenth Century* (New York: D. Appelton and Company, 1901), 103, 130, 132.

9 Murphy, "Voyages from Holland to America," 25.

10 This waterway has never been adequately identified.

11 Murphy, "Voyages from Holland to America," 25.

12 G. Troost, "Extracts from the Voyage of De Vries," *Collections of the New York Historical Society*, Second Series, vol. I, (New York: H. Ludwig, 1841): 243–80.

13 J. Moulton, *History of the State of New York*, vol. I (New York: E. Bliss and E. White Publishers, 1826).

14 T. F. Gordon, *The History of New Jersey from its Discovery by Europeans to the Adoption of the Constitution* (Trenton: T. Fenton, 1834).

15 Moulton, *History of the State of New York*, 416.

16 Murphy, "Voyages from Holland to America."

17 The language relating to the event in the Murphy translation of 1857 is almost identical to that of Troost.

18 J. Moulton, *History of the State of New York*, 417–18.

19 T. F. Gordon, *The History of New*, 9.

20 For this plot device to work, all the native peoples in the story have to belong to one tribe, the Lenni-Lenape.

21 Whether, in fact, Pocahontas actually saved Capt. John Smith's life has been questioned for many years by a variety of authorities. Helen Rountree, *Pocahontas's People: The Powhatan Indians of Virginia Through Four Centuries* (Norman: University of Oklahoma Press, 1990), 38.

22 Robert Dale Owen, *Pocahontas: A Historical Drama in Five Acts* (New York: George Dearborn, 1837).

23 Paula A. Gunn. *Pocahontas: Medicine Woman, Spy, Entrepreneur, Diplomat* (New York: HarperCollins, 2004).

24 Ella Dorsey, *Pocahontas* (Washington, DC: The Howard Press, 1906), 4.

25 VanWyck Brooks, *The World of Washington Irving* (New York: E. P. Dutton & Co., 1944), 192.

26 John W. Barber and Henry Howe, *Historical Collections of the State of New Jersey* (New Haven: Justus H. Bradley, 1844), 204.

27 Isaac Mickle, *Reminiscences of Old Gloucester or Incidents in the History of the Counties of Gloucester, Atlantic and Camden, New Jersey* (Philadelphia: Townsend Ward, 1845).

28 Ibid., 2.

29 Ibid., 4–5. Note that almost identical language was used by Dorsey in 1906 to describe Pocahontas.

30 John R. Brodhead, *History of the State of New York*, vol. II (New York: Harper Brothers, 1871).

31 Ibid., 225.

32 Frank R. Stockton, *Stories of New Jersey* (New York: American Book Company, 1896), 22.

33 There is no ethnographic evidence to support Stockton's contention that women alone exercised peace diplomacy in native societies of the mid-Atlantic region. While Stockton may have been alluding to the matrilineal structure of many of these native societies (Lenni-Lenape and Iroquois among them), which afforded women a great deal more power in their respective societies than was the case in American society at the time, it is more likely that he was anachronistically projecting his own thinking into the past.

34 Stockton, *Stories of New Jersey*, 22–23.

35 Ida Mae Roeder, "Young Indian Mother Risked Life in Camden to Save White Crew," *Courier-Post* (Camden, New Jersey), January 23, 1953, 8.

36 Howard M. Cooper, *Historical Sketches of Camden, N.J.* (Camden: Horace B. Kelter, 1909).

37 Ibid., 68.

38 Ibid., 67.

39 Ibid., 68.

40 Archivegrid, "Joseph W. Moulton papers, ca. 1820–ca. 1875," accessed May 25, 2017, https://beta.worldcat.org/archivegrid/record.php?id=58780190.

41 Joseph J. Felcone, *New Jersey Books, 1801–1860*, vol. II, (Princeton: Joseph, J. Felcone, Inc., 1996), 272–73.

42 Ibid.

43 Barber's *Connecticut Historical Collections* is generally credited with being the first popular history book in the United States, ignoring Gordon's state history of 1834, which targeted a general audience.

44 Barber and Howe, *Historical Collections of the State of New Jersey*, Preface.

45 Philip Mackey, *A Gentleman of Much Promise: The Diary of Isaac Mickle, 1837–1845* (Philadelphia: University of Pennsylvania Press, 1977), 278–79; 439.

46 Ibid., 278.

47 Mackey, *A Gentleman of Much Promise*, 474, 488–89, 494.

48 Two years after publishing *Stories of New Jersey*, Stockton published another historical work: *Buccaneers of Our Coasts* (London: Macmillian Company, 1898).

49 Edwin Bowen, "Frank R. Stockton," in *The Sewanee Review* 11, no. 4 (1903), 474–78.

50 Edwin Bowen, "The Fiction of Frank R. Stockton," in *The Sewanee Review* 28, no. 3 (1920), 456.

51 Emily Cooper Johnson, "Introduction," in *Historical Sketch of Camden* (Camden: H. Carpenter, 1931).

52 Ibid., xviii.

53 Ibid.

54 This was an approach common to historians of the nineteenth century. Mark A. Weinstein, "The Creative Imagination in Fiction and History," *Genre* 9 (1976): 263–77. Several of the authors reviewed here also made clear their thinking that the purpose of understanding the past is to instruct the present. James Macauley, *The Natural, Statistical and Civil History of the State of New York* (Albany: Gould & Banks and William Gould & Co., 1829), Preface; Barber and Howe, *Historical Collections of the State of New Jersey*, 4; Mickle, *Reminiscences of Old Gloucester*, Preface.

55 Gordon, *The History of New Jersey*, Preface.

56 Charles Joline, "Introduction," in *Historical Sketches of Camden, N.J.* (Camden: H. Carpenter, 1909), 3. Charles VanDyke Joline (1851–?) studied law with Peter Voorhees of Camden as did Howard Cooper and together with Cooper was a founding member of the Camden County Bar Association. George R. Prowell, *History of Camden County, New Jersey* (Philadelphia: L. J. Richards & Company, 1883), 231.

57 David Levin, *History as Romantic Art: Bancroft, Prescott, Motley, and Parkman* (New York: AMS Press, 1967).

58 Ibid., 28.

59 T. Babbington McCaulay, *Essays, Critical and Miscellaneous* (Philadelphia: Carey and Hart, 1847), 55.

60 The philosopher George Hegel (1770–1831) also espoused this teleological view of history, although with a different end point. It would not be challenged until the publication of Herbert Butterfield, *The Whig Interpretation of History* (London: G. Bell, London, 1931).

61 Mackey, *A Gentleman of Much Promise*, 169.

62 George W. Stocking Jr., *Race, Culture and Evolution* (Chicago: University of Chicago Press, 1968), 119.

63 Ibid., 249–59.

64 Nancy F. Cox, *The Grounding of Modern Feminism* (New Haven: Yale University Press, 1987). Corrine M. McConnaughy, *The Woman Suffrage Movement in America: A Reassessment* (New York: Cambridge University Press, 2013).

65 Patricia Okker, *Our Sister Editors: Sarah J. Hale and the Tradition of Nineteenth-Century American Women Editors* (Athens: The University of Georgia Press, 1995), 77.

66 Philadelphia Yearly Meeting, "Schism and Reform Circa 1800–1900," accessed May 18, 2017, http://www.pym.org/faith-and-practice/historical-introduction/3-schism-and-reform-circa-1800-1900/. See also Philadelphia Yearly Meeting, "Reconciliation Circa 1900–1955," accessed May 18, 2017, http://www.pym.org/faith-and-practice/historical-introduction/3-schism-and-reform-circa-1800-1900/.

67 Ibid.

68 John D. F. Morgan and Samuel H. Richards, "Early Activities in the Upper Four Tenths," *Camden County Historical Publications* 3, no. 1 (1948), accessed May 18, 2017, http://www.dvrbs.com/camden-texts/CamdenNJ-CCHS-Upper410.htm.

69 Robert A. Shinn and Kevin Cook, *Along the Cooper River, Camden to Haddonfield* (Charleston, SC: Carolina Arcadia Publishing, 2014), 11.

70 Gordon S. Wood, *The Purpose of the Past: Reflections on the Uses of History* (New York: The Penguin Press, 2008).

71 Defined as the projection of present-day ideas and perspectives into depictions or interpretations of the past.

72 E. H. Carr, *What is History?* (Cambridge, England: Cambridge University Press, 1961).

ADDITIONAL SOURCES

de Chateaubriand, François-René. "Atala," In *Atala, Indian Cottage, Idyls & First Navigator* (London: Walker & Edwards, 1817), 1–72.

de Vries, David Pieterzen. *Korte Historiael ende Journaels Aenteyckeninge van Verscheyden Voyagiens in de Vier Deelen des Wereldts-ronde, als Europa, Africa, Asia, ende Amerika gedaen* (Alkmaar, Netherlands: Symon Cornelisz Bekegreeft, 1655).

Visscher, Nicolaes and Petrus Schenk, *Novi Belgii Novæque Angliæ nec non Partis Virginiæ Tabula: Multis in Locis Emendata*, Accessed April 3, 2017, https://www.loc.gov/item/2001621332/.

Publications of the South Jersey Culture & History Center

When you purchase these titles:
All profits from book purchases support future publications about the culture and history of South Jersey.

SoJourn 1.1 Spring 2016
SoJourn 1.2 Winter 2016/17
SoJourn 2.1 Summer 2017

Early Recollections and Life of Dr. James Still by James Still

William Still: His Life and Work to This Time by James P. Boyd

The Outfit by Budd Wilson

Bungalow Life in the Pines: Letters of Fred Noyes Senior, collected by Judy Courter

Herbert Payne: Last of the Old-Time Charcoal Makers and His Coaling Process by Ted Gordon

Swan Bay Jim / Gasoline Seventeen Cents a Gallon; Moonshine a Dollar a Quart by Gary B. Giberson

Burlington Biographies: A History of Burlington, New Jersey, Told Through the Lives and Times of Its People by Robert L. Thompson

Garment Workers of South Jersey: Nine Oral Histories, preface by Dr. Lisa E. Cox; introduction by Patricia A. Martinelli

A Trip to Mars by Charles K. Landis

Seasons by Dallas Lore Sharp

Atlantic City: Its Early & Modern History by Alexander Barrington Irvine ("Carnesworthe")

Pine Barrens: Life and Legends by Tom Kinsella and Paul W. Schopp

Forthcoming
Everyday Adventures by Samuel Scoville Jr.

With Eager Hands: The Life of Elizabeth Coleman White by Albertine Senske

For more information about these titles, visit our website: www.stockton.edu/sjchc/

Thank you for supporting our efforts.

Calico or Dobbin's Bog

Richard Watson

Many Pine Barrens explorers have ventured up along the Oswego stream in Bass River Township to see what remains of the old bog-iron furnace town of Martha. Embarking from the ruins of the former paper manufactory at Harrisville, the intent traveler can follow a gently winding sand road beyond the eastern side of the mill pond to discover the fenced site of a furnace that once prospered when ironmaking was a major industry throughout the pinewoods of South Jersey.

Built by Pennsylvania ironmaster Isaac Potts in about 1793,[1] Martha Furnace would remain a thriving concern for more than 50 years. Even today, the area where this old ironworks once stood contrasts dramatically with the surrounding woods. Visitors will likely distinguish the non-native trees at the location, and further investigations may uncover the cellar hole from the ironmaster's house as well as the remains of the dam and raceway that had provided power to the enterprise. Most travelers to the site then decide to return along the same route on which they arrived; however, some of the more intrepid have pressed on beyond Martha Furnace in search of other places that have also been swallowed by the pines. Among the forgotten sites that the excursionist may seek to explore is a small, vanished village known as Calico.

The path that leads away from Martha toward the east was a well-traveled road connecting that formerly busy furnace town to nearby Tuckerton, or Clamtown, as it was also known. Along that route, as the underbrush closes in, the narrowing sand road crosses a gated access lane to an extensive and still active chain of cranberry bogs along the Beaver Run stream. These cranberry meadows and the small village that grew up around them were called

Calico, though that name had been attached to the cedar swamps, lowlands, and pine woods in the vicinity since the very beginning of the nineteenth century, when the nearby Martha Furnace was a place of great activity.

The cultivated cranberry meadows at Calico are among the oldest in that section of the Pine Barrens and date to just after the Civil War, when agriculturalists feverishly purchased once worthless swampland all throughout southern New Jersey and developed the parcels for the cultivation of the prized and valuable red fruit. Countless enterprising men and speculators would fall victim to the so-called "cranberry craze."[2,3] One man who caught the cranberry fever was an industrious farmer and rising politician from Mount Holly named Samuel Dobbins, who would not only tame this small area of the Pines, but would later become a respected United States Congressman. His tale is at the very heart of the Calico story.

The first documentary account of Calico may be a singular and brief mention of the place in the so-called *Martha Furnace Diary*,[4] which chronicled daily events at

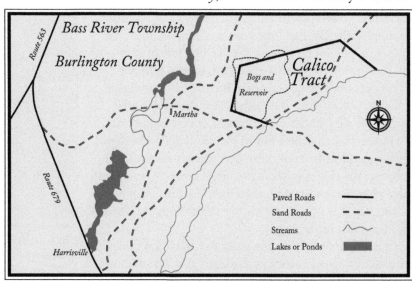

Map courtesy of Richard Watson.

Today the Cutts family continues to grow cranberries on the bogs at Calico. Samuel Dobbins first established these meadows in 1866. *Courtesy of Richard Watson.*

the ironworks between the years 1808 and 1815. A June 6, 1809, entry in that journal states, "Peter Cox went out to Calico & whipped Jack Johnson."[5] It was likely this lone reference, coupled with the close proximity of the two localities on later maps, that led early researchers to guess that Calico was a residential village appurtenant to the ironworks at Martha.[6]

Historians presumably accessed old tax duplicates to further fuel their speculation about Calico's past, but just how significant the place was to the furnace operation seems to be something of a mystery. Even the exact location of the site had long been a point of conjecture among investigators. Though the sketchy tale of Calico's connection to Martha Furnace has been told and retold over the years,[7, 8] evidence for an iron-era village at Calico is very thin. The earliest available maps offer nothing to substantiate a settlement, contemporary to the ironworks, anywhere but in the immediate vicinity of the furnace. Furthermore, property records seem to confirm that the tiny community named Calico arose several years after iron production ceased at Martha. Despite its questionable origin, the history of this long forgotten spot is no less intriguing.

The chain of title for the sizeable Calico tract does provide some insight into its shadowy past. The 442 acre parcel was situated just east of the operation at Martha and the vast furnace lands surrounded Calico on all sides.

Indeed, the Calico tract was originally part of the extensive furnace lands, but when Isaac Potts, the original ironmaster, sold the works to four investors in 1798, he reserved the right of soil to this particular lot, conveying the privilege to mine the ore on the property to Martha's new owners. Noted historian Charles S. Boyer cited this conveyance in his work, *Early Forges and Furnaces in New Jersey,*[10] but it would appear he was unaware that the property in question was the enigmatic Calico Tract.

Several years after the furnace was sold, Isaac's son, Edward Potts, acquired the Calico property from his father.[11] In that deed, the rights of the nearby furnace owners are described as follows:

> Excepting and reserving out of this present grant unto George Ashbridge, Charles Shoemaker, Morris Robeson and John Paul, their several and respective heirs and assigns forever all the ore that now is or hereafter may be in or upon the said above described tract of land and also all the timber, trees and woods now growing or that may hereafter grow upon the said described tract of land with liberty of ingress, egress, and regress as well for the purpose of digging for and taking away the ore and of cutting down, felling and hauling away all the timber, trees, and woods as for the purpose of passage in, upon, and over

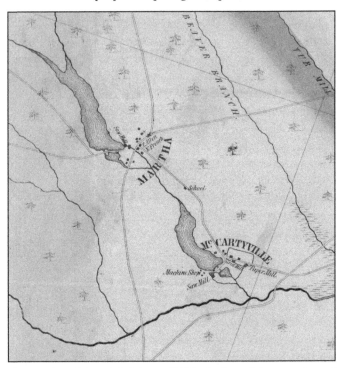

This portion of the 1849 Otley and Whiteford map[9] shows no formal settlement in the vicinity of the Beaver Branch. Though the iron era in the Jersey Pines was ending at this time, it appears unlikely that a substantial worker's village existed at Calico while Martha Furnace was in operation.

the said tract with or without horses, cattle, carts, waggons or other carriages to and from all and every or any part or parts of the lands of them the said George Ashbridge, Charles Shoemaker, Morris Robeson and John Paul which rights and privileges the said Isaac Potts hath heretofore sold and conveyed to them.

During the heyday of iron production along the Oswego, this piece of pine land and cedar swamp in southern New Jersey would remain in the hands of the Potts family, despite their Philadelphia residence. It would be Edward's son, Isaac W. Potts, the grandson of the furnace's founder, who would eventually dispose of the property on the first day of December 1836.[12] Even in that conveyance, a covenant reserving the rights to the iron ore for the Martha Furnace Company remained attached to the property.

The fact that Isaac Potts chose to reserve this particular piece of land along Beaver Run is curious to be sure. One can only speculate what significance the Potts exclusion had to the furnace operation at Martha during that time. It was, after all, the period when some have suggested an active community of ironworkers made their residence at Calico, but those who purport that much of Martha's labor force lived in a village there fail to cite any evidence to substantiate that claim. More than likely, Calico and other places like Sassafras that were just as inconspicuously mentioned in the furnace diary, were simply ore-bed locations or coaling sites that helped Martha satisfy its enormous appetite for raw materials.

Maybe some crude and transient accommodations existed for the colliers (charcoal makers) and ore diggers in the vicinity, but nothing in the deed records for the property supports the idea that a village existed at Calico to house the men who worked at the proximate furnace. Indeed, when Isaac W. Potts sold the property to area resident William Allen, the legal description made

Catalpa trees betray one of the old home sites at Calico. *Courtesy of Richard Watson.*

no mention of improvements to the property. Despite the considerable sum of $750 that Allen paid, the transaction would appear to have secured him a "certain tract of pineland" and not much else.[13]

William Allen's ownership of the Calico tract would not last long and it is curious that just four years later, on August 29, 1840, he would sell the property to Isaiah Stackhouse for only $200.[14] Not the best investment it would seem, though clearly there is more to the story. In the Pines, the value of land was judged according to the extent of quality timber on the property, and Allen would have wasted little time in logging his new acquisition. There was also a widespread financial crisis occurring at the time that may have contributed to the significant drop in value. Or maybe it was the "great conflagration" that swept through the area in August of 1838 that laid waste to the property. Newspapers at the time described the wildfire, which began on the Martha Furnace tract, as "the greatest calamity of the kind ever known there," and losses were estimated at $100,000.[15]

The South Jersey iron industry collapsed in the 1840s, and, shortly thereafter, the furnace at Martha went out of blast forever.[16] It is believed that the making of charcoal, once so vital to the manufacture of iron, may have continued for a short period,[17] and perhaps the few people who remained in the area were able to eke out a living on the surrounding lands, tending the coal pits or hauling the finished product to a landing on the river below Harrisville. The undertakings that attempted to fill the vacuum left by the closing of Martha Furnace, however, would not long endure. In 1855, a correspondent for the *Mount Holly Mirror* visited Martha Furnace and reported on the activities in that vicinity:

> The timber, so long the main support of the region, is gone. The primitive and second growths of pine and cedar have disappeared and [with] that the wood chopping and swamping business is comparatively ended; and that from stern necessity, farming is now the dominant idea. Several captains of vessels have already disposed of their charcoal boats, and have turned to reclaiming old sand fields and grubbing up oak scrubs and whortleberry bushes preparatory to seeding.[18]

In fact, a few adventurous souls had already settled in the neighborhood, hoping to scrape out a living from the inauspicious pinewoods. Just around the corner from the Calico tract, Ellis Adams had purchased a 42.5 acre parcel from William Williams in 1845.[19] Soon thereafter, Adams erected a humble homestead and cleared the surrounding land, creating a modest farm just south of the Beaver Run stream. It was this locality that Henry Beck somewhat erroneously memorialized as Calico in his *Forgotten Towns* books, when he explored the vanished places in the Pines during the 1930s.[20] Edward Perry, from Mullica Township, purchased that "certain farm and premises" from Ellis Adams in 1866 and, for a time, the place was known a Perry Field.[21]

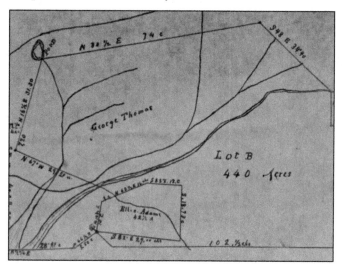

By the early 1900s, George Thomas operated the bogs at Calico. The Ellis Adams property is shown south of Beaver Run and opposite the Calico Tract. The image above is a portion of Green's Map of Chetwood, which George Thomas drafted in 1912.

As activities in and about Martha declined, Isaiah Stackhouse maintained ownership of his lands at nearby Calico. By 1849, he found a willing buyer, and sold the large parcel to Thomas Morey, a neighbor from old Washington Township.[22] Morey's $300 purchase of the property would begin a residence at Calico that spanned nearly a half-century. Though it is certainly possible that Stackhouse made some effort to cultivate the land during his ownership, it was probably Morey who built an unassuming home and continued to clear the property, carving out a small truck farm for his family along Beaver Run. An old roadway crossed the Beaver Branch in the vicinity of the Morey farm and, for a time, the neighborhood became known as Cedar Causeway.

The challenges associated with bringing this wild land into some reasonable state of cultivation must have proven formidable. Additional difficulties would soon face Morey. Less than six years after purchasing the land, former owner Stackhouse initiated a lawsuit against Morey for failure to honor the purchase agreement. The Circuit Court of Burlington County ruled against Morey and awarded Stackhouse the $250 owed him.[23] Morey could not satisfy the debt, which resulted in a court-ordered sale. Burlington County Sheriff Samuel A. Dobbins soon advertised to auction the property.

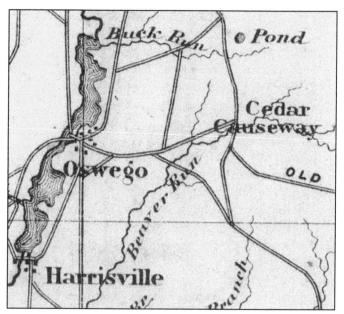

The location of Cedar Causeway is depicted on this map of Burlington County by F. W. Beers. It was in this area that Thomas Morey established a farm in the mid-1800s.

SHERIFF'S SALE

By virtue of a writ issued out of the Circuit Court of Burlington County, I will expose to sale at public vendue, on Monday the 16th of July, between the hours of 12 and 5 o'clock, P.M., on the premises, at the residence of the defendant, in Washington Township, Burlington County, one mile from Martha Furnace, all the right, title and interest of the said defendant in all that tract of Pine Land and Cedar Swamp, situate as aforesaid, containing 442 acres, adjoining the lands of Wm. Allen, Esq., Mrs. French and others—being the same tract of land which was conveyed by Isaiah Stackhouse to the defendant and wife by deed duly executed and recorded.

Seized as the property of Thomas Morey, defendant, taken in execution at the suit of Isaiah Stackhouse, plaintiff, and to be sold by SAMUEL A. DOBBINS, Sheriff.

June 16, 1855[24]

On August 21, 1855, Samuel N. Haines, from Mount Holly, purchased the property for $205.[25] It is clear that Morey had made some improvements to the tract during his time there as the advertisement above states the sale would occur "at the residence of the defendant" and the subsequent conveyance to Haines was for all that above-mentioned pine land and farmland.

Curiously, Sheriff Dobbins acquired a half-interest in the Calico tract for $300 just months after Haines purchased the parcel.[26] Exactly what plans Dobbins and Haines had for the property at that time is unknown. Perhaps the promise of a future rail line through the area enticed them to speculate in the land. In any case, the two men soon divided the property, with Dobbins receiving 179 acres on the westerly side and Haines retaining the balance. Despite this partition, the whole parcel remained identified as the Dobbins-Haines Calico Tract when Francis B. Chetwood surveyed the surrounding Martha Furnace lands in the late 1850s.[27] Neither Dobbins nor Haines apparently had any intention of settling on these wild lands in the far-away Pines. One might even wonder whether the new owners allowed Thomas Morey to stay on the land and continue to work the farm he had built there, for as we will see, his days at Calico had not yet ended.

SAMUEL DOBBINS AND THE NEW JERSEY CRANBERRY COMPANY

Samuel Atkinson Dobbins was born into a well-known and long-established family from Vincentown, Burlington County, on April 14, 1814. As a young man, he attended the public schools and worked beside his father on the family farm. At age 22, young Dobbins married Damaris Harker and looked toward his own endeavors in agriculture. To that end, he and his wife moved near Mount Holly in 1838, where, along the road to Lumberton, Dobbins achieved his dream of establishing his own farm. Undoubtedly ambitious, it would later be said he cleared more than 500 acres of forest in his lifetime, converting it into productive agricultural land. His hard work, and the prosperity that followed, brought Dobbins a good deal of respect, and he soon became recognized as a man of great character and integrity.

By 1846, Dobbins had entered politics, serving on township committees for several years before filling the polled position of a Chosen Freeholder. Subsequently, the Whigs of Burlington County elected him High Sheriff, a position that he occupied for a three-year period, beginning in 1854. Voters subsequently elected Dobbins to three terms in the State General Assembly,

Samuel Atkinson Dobbins. *Photograph by Mathew Brady.*

where he served on a variety of important committees including Agriculture. In 1864, he attended the Republican National Convention as a delegate and, in 1872, he entered the United States Congress as an elected representative of the New Jersey Second Congressional District. Samuel Dobbins served in the Forty-third and Forty-fourth Congresses from 1873 to 1877, but declined to seek re-election at the conclusion of these terms, preferring to resume his agricultural pursuits.[28]

When Dobbins and Haines acquired the Calico tract, a portion of the property comprised the type of lowlands where the treasured cranberry thrived. By the 1850s, some efforts at improving the wild Jersey meadows had begun, and like the cranberry pioneers from Cape Cod who had started several decades earlier, a few adventurous Jersey men began experimenting with the systematic cultivation of the cranberry in hopes the endeavor would prove remunerative. To be sure, the successes of early growers like William R. Braddock near Indian Mills in Shamong Township and Joseph Hinchman at Taunton in Medford generated a great deal of excitement among those who owned suitable land and the means to improve it. Interest in the incipient industry continued to build and soon a full-blown cranberry craze had commenced, causing once worthless land in and around the Pines to command unimaginable sums from investors hoping for grand profits.

Even along the Wading River, early efforts to cultivate the cranberry soon began. Articles in journals like *The Working Farmer* described the suitability of the Oswego Lands for raising cranberries, and they detailed the successes of several pioneer growers there.[29] Dobbins must have been enticed by such encouraging accounts and, at some point, he began to develop plans to improve his cranberry land at Calico.

In the spring of 1866, this prominent farmer from Mount Holly acquired the other half-interest in the property for $1000 from Isaac Haines,[30] who had inherited the land after the death of his brother, Samuel.[31] When it came to cultivating cranberries at Calico, however, Dobbins had no interest in going it alone. Unlike in Massachusetts, many of the cranberry bogs in New Jersey were built with funds raised by the incorporation of capital stock companies. Scores of these enterprises were established in the prosperous years immediately following the Civil War. It would be in this manner that cranberry bogs along Beaver Run would come to be built, and an interesting series of transactions would help Dobbins see his vision fulfilled.

Little more than a month after acquiring sole ownership of the Calico Tract, Dobbins sold a 129 acre part of his original acquisition for $1290 to investor and future business partner, Benjamin Franklin.[32] This purchase represented much of the northwestern portion of the property, being the area where cultivated cranberry bogs would soon be constructed. Franklin, oddly enough, was an Episcopal minister who resided in Burlington at the time. One can only guess what prompted this clergyman to speculate in the emergent cranberry business, but the transaction shows that few could resist the promise of great riches from cranberries. Dobbins then divided other parts of the tract into saleable lots and soon found willing buyers for several parcels.

The year 1866, however, would mark more than just a flurry of land deals at Calico. On the first of September, Samuel Dobbins and Benjamin Franklin would partner with James Lippincott to file the necessary papers to incorporate the New Jersey Cranberry Company.[33] Lippincott, like Dobbins, hailed from Mount Holly and operated as a surveyor and real estate agent. On November 8, the business received its official charter and authorization to issue $20,000 of capital stock. The 129 acres that Franklin purchased from Dobbins just months earlier was sold to this new venture for a handsome profit, though Franklin likely received shares of company stock in lieu of cash for his land. Whatever the arrangement, Franklin ended up with just less than half of the issued stock while Lippincott held a quarter-interest in the company. Dobbins' share was probably slightly less than Lippincott's, as subsequent stock transfers suggest he may have held 45 of the 200 shares issued.[34] A few friends or family members may have held minority interests in the company as well.

As the New Jersey Cranberry Company developed the bogs at Calico, its owners soon realized that one essential requirement for cranberry culture remained scarce. The Beaver Run stream bypassed these newly

constructed bogs to the south and the supply of water to the recently improved meadows proved inadequate. So, in 1868, Dobbins sold a small 3.75 acre parcel of his remaining land at Calico to the New Jersey Cranberry Company for $50.[35] The conveyed lot was quite unique as it measured but 2 rods (33 feet) wide, though its length extended for more than a mile. On that ground, workmen dug a canal from Beaver Run for supplying much-needed water to the company's bogs. Clearly identified on maps from that time and easily located today, that canal is particularly interesting because it defines the northern and eastern boundary for the original Calico tract. Even today, explorers can discover the dry ditch where it intersects the Calico-Warren Grove Road, not far from its intersection with the old Shamong Road.

These mounds of sand along the road to Warren Grove mark the location of a lengthy canal which was dug in 1868 to supply water to the New Jersey Cranberry Company Bogs. *Courtesy of Richard Watson.*

It has been said that nine out of ten early attempts at cranberry cultivation failed,[36] and while the bogs at Calico seems to have held some promise at the beginning, the enterprise probably never met the lofty expectations of its first owners. By the mid-1870s, Benjamin Franklin had moved to Shrewsbury and, about that time, began transferring his surely discounted shares in the company to relatives.[37] Over the next twenty years, he slowly divested himself of the business with most of his shares passing to his daughter, Emma W. Van Vliet. At the same time, Dobbins' political responsibilities, first as a State Representative and later as a United States Congressman, must have distracted him from the bogs in Bass River Township. While he did return to agricultural pursuits for a few years, it is unknown to what extent these bogs offered remuneration. The third partner, James Lippincott, retained his interest in the company throughout this period and, at some point, took over the responsibilities of treasurer for the corporation.[38]

Bankbook entries for the New Jersey Cranberry Company in 1866. *Courtesy of Richard Watson.*

Samuel Atkinson Dobbins died on May 26, 1886, and his interest in the New Jersey Cranberry Company (45 shares) passed to his son, Samuel A. Dobbins Jr. James Lippincott retained his interest in the company, but, in 1896, appears to have brokered a deal whereby Samuel Dobbins Jr. received the bulk of Franklin's original shares in the company from the Van Vliets. This purchase, along with a few shares he had acquired prior to his father's death, gave Dobbins a majority interest in the company as he now held 120 of the 200 outstanding shares. The younger Dobbins apparently had little interest in growing cranberries, however, and soon looked to rid himself of such responsibilities.

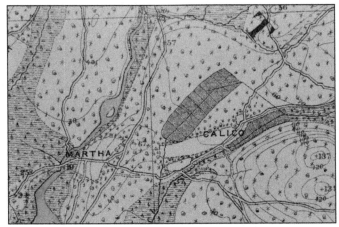

This map, completed by Cornelius Clarkson Vermeule for the Geological Survey of New Jersey, shows the New Jersey Cranberry Company's bogs at Calico. The straight canal dug from Beaver Run to the cranberry meadows is the Northeast border of the Calico tract. The cleared fields are associated with several farms that were established at Calico.

The Village of Calico

As noted above, when Dobbins began looking for partners in developing his cranberry bogs on the western portion of the Calico tract in 1866, he also divided much of the remaining land into smaller lots he offered for sale. All of these plots straddled the road that led to Warren Grove and bordered the Beaver Run stream to the south. On July 20, 1866, Thomas Morey, who more than a decade earlier had owned the entire parcel, bought just over sixteen acres for $162.40 from Dobbins,[39] and, two years later, added an adjoining pie-shaped lot to his earlier purchase.[40] Morey's acquisition presumably included part of the original farm that he had established earlier at Calico, but he was not the only person to buy lots there. On the same day that Morey bought his first piece, a man named George Ryan purchased just less than 20 acres for $10 an acre.[41] This parcel adjoined the land that Franklin had purchased, and like the others, bounded Beaver Run to the south. The following year, Ryan purchased an adjacent lot,[42] giving him a contig-

uous tract of more than 46 acres on which he built a house and established a farm. Over the next several years, Dobbins sold additional small lots. Deeds of neighboring property indicate that Joseph McNinney (possibly McAnney) bought a parcel at Calico, but that lot's northeastern boundary is not known. Thomas Morey's wife, Phebe, also bought two parcels at Calico[43] and his son, J. Kenneth Morey, purchased a small piece as well.[44]

To a careful explorer, the locations of the Morey and Ryan homesteads can still be pinpointed today, and the remains of at least one other possible dwelling can be located nearby as well. These farms, along with the neighboring Ellis Adams place, must have assuredly comprised the heart of this tiny pineland village called Calico that would eventually appear on maps of the area.

When renowned folklorist Henry Charlton Beck visited the ruins around Calico in the 1930s, he surmised that the former buildings were attendant to the cranberry bogs in the vicinity, and his speculation may well have been correct.[45] Dobbins must have known that cranberry bogs required careful tending and oversight. Surely he

The Thomas Morey homestead sat beside this pond formed by the damming of the Beaver Branch. *Courtesy of Richard Watson.*

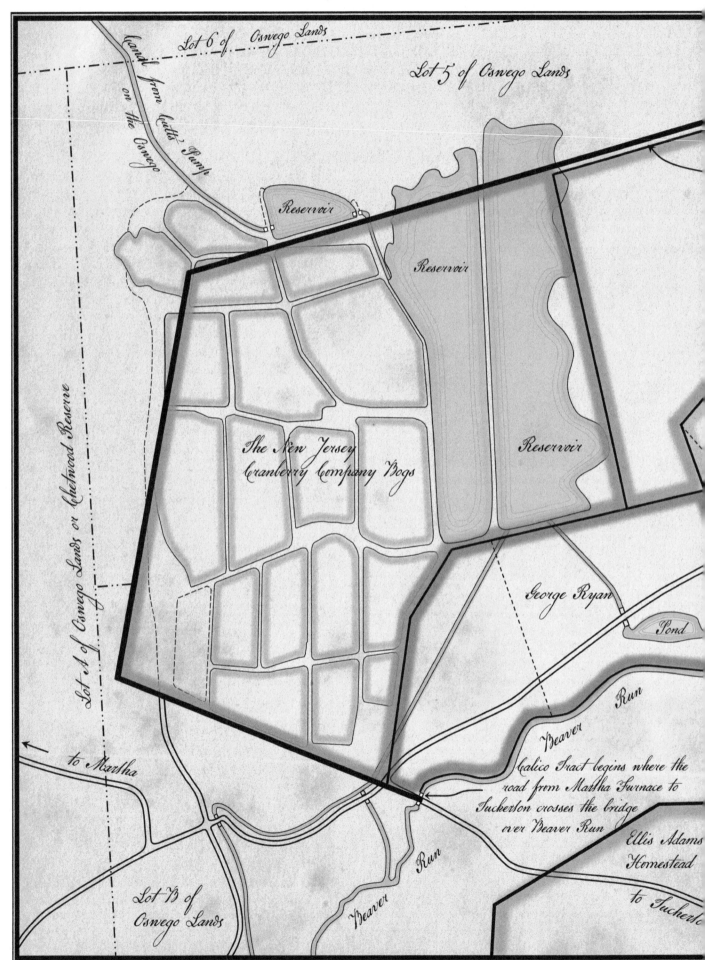

Lot 6 of Oswego Lands

Lot 5 of Oswego Lands

Canal from Watts Swamp on the Oswego

Reservoir

Reservoir

Reservoir

The New Jersey Cranberry Company Bogs

Lot A of Oswego Lands or Chetwood Reserve

George Ryan

Pond

Run

Beaver

to Martha

Calico Tract begins where the road from Martha Furnace to Tuckerton crosses the bridge over Beaver Run

Lot B of Oswego Lands

Beaver Run

Ellis Adams Homestead

to Tuckerton

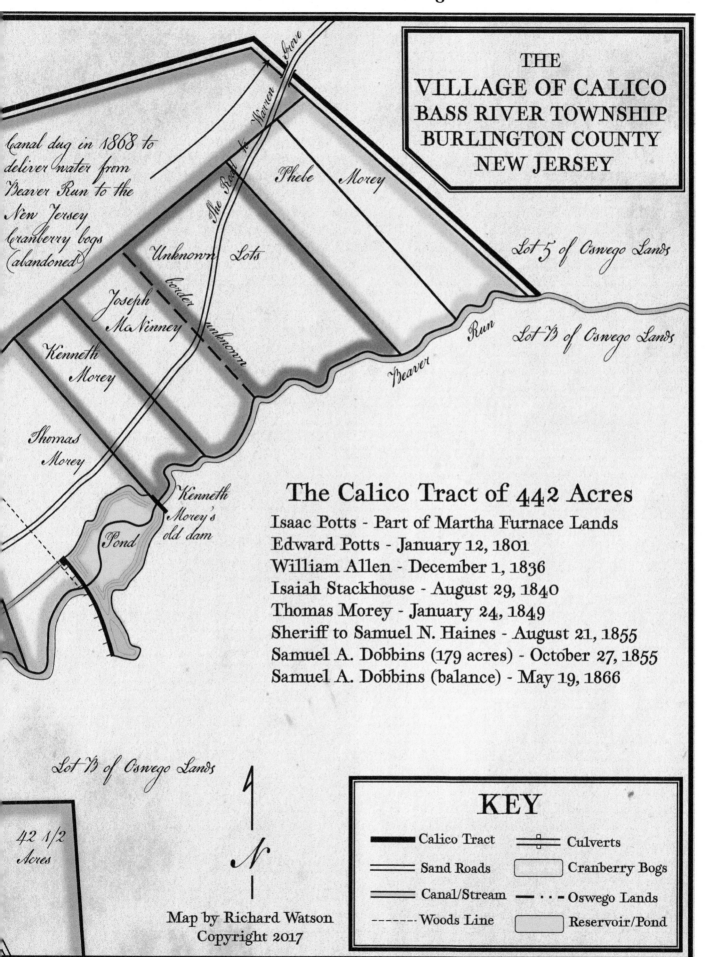

THE
VILLAGE OF CALICO
BASS RIVER TOWNSHIP
BURLINGTON COUNTY
NEW JERSEY

Canal dug in 1868 to deliver water from Beaver Run to the New Jersey Cranberry bogs (abandoned)

The Road to Warren

Grove

Phebe Morey

Lot 5 of Oswego Lands

Unknown Lots

Joseph McNinney

border unknown

Kenneth Morey

Beaver   *Run*

Lot B of Oswego Lands

Thomas Morey

Kenneth Morey's old dam

Pond

The Calico Tract of 442 Acres

Isaac Potts - Part of Martha Furnace Lands
Edward Potts - January 12, 1801
William Allen - December 1, 1836
Isaiah Stackhouse - August 29, 1840
Thomas Morey - January 24, 1849
Sheriff to Samuel N. Haines - August 21, 1855
Samuel A. Dobbins (179 acres) - October 27, 1855
Samuel A. Dobbins (balance) - May 19, 1866

Lot B of Oswego Lands

42 1/2 Acres

N

Map by Richard Watson
Copyright 2017

KEY

▬▬	Calico Tract	▤	Culverts
═	Sand Roads	▭	Cranberry Bogs
─	Canal/Stream	▬ · · ·	Oswego Lands
- - - -	Woods Line	▨	Reservoir/Pond

would have enlisted local men from the area to work on the bogs at different times of the year. Though both Morey and Ryan toiled with small truck farms on their property, census records identify them as laborers who likely found work on the nearby Calico bogs.

The Morey family probably engaged in their own efforts growing cranberries, too. Thomas Morey, along with his wife and son, owned much of the property along the Beaver Run stream itself. Early topographic maps suggest that bogs existed along that stream just above the Morey farm and later deeds refer to Kenneth Morey's old dam across Beaver Run.

There is also a rather grizzly tale that surrounds Calico's longtime resident, Thomas Morey, whose infamous actions traveled far beyond the remote Jersey woods and appeared in the pages of newspapers published in Trenton, Philadelphia, and even New York. Toward the end of August 1887, *The Philadelphia Inquirer* reported on an aged farmer shooting a vegetable thief living in the village of Calico, Burlington County.[46] The paper stated that several farmers in the area had recently experienced the loss of potatoes, corn, and other truck from their fields, supposedly at the hands of a pitiable neighbor named Abel Broom. Broom was described as wretchedly poor, living with his wife and five children in a one-room hovel on a small lot adjoining the farm of Thomas Morey. The report states that about daybreak on August 23, the 79-year-old Morey lay in wait at the edge of his field when the shiftless Broom arrived to help himself to his neighbor's produce. Morey then approached the man and knocked him down with the butt of his shotgun. Pleading with the angry man, Broom tried to escape, but as he reached the fence separating the properties, he was struck by a load of shot in the hip and groin. The story recounts how Broom's wife heard his cries and came to his rescue, dragging the limp body of her wounded husband home.

The newspaper describes how the next morning, Broom's wife appealed for help from Justice Adams in nearby Bass River. After traveling the short distance to Calico, Adams took a statement from the badly injured man, but was not inclined to arrest Morey at the time, suggesting that perhaps an inquest should be held. Dissatisfied with the inaction of the local justice, another family member traveled to Hammonton later that day to beg a lawyer for assistance. Counselor John J. Walsh immediately drove to Calico and succeeded in securing an arrest order for Morey from a justice of the peace in nearby Lower Bank. Morey was taken into custody and transported to the jail in Mount Holly. Walsh also called for a doctor to examine Broom. After attending

to the stricken man, the physician thought it unlikely that the patient would recover from his wounds. Within a matter of days, Broom succumbed to his injuries.

A subsequent and conflicting article claims that Morey and Broom had quarreled for some time over the rights to a large chestnut tree that straddled the property line.[47] This account claims that Broom's body was found badly beaten beneath the tree, apparently by a club found nearby. Morey, the article says, brought news of the murder to Broom's family in hopes of casting suspicion on others but he was soon arrested as the culprit.

In those days, justice was swift. By the end of October, the papers reported that Morey, who had recently changed his plea to guilty, would soon be sentenced.[48] The following piece appeared in the November 17 issue of *The Weekly Trenton Times*:

> Thomas Morey, with tears in his eyes and his form bent with age, stood up in the courtroom at Mount Holly yesterday to receive the judgement of the law for shooting and killing Abel Broom at Bass River last August. The defendant, who is eighty years old, said: "I didn't mean to kill Broom," and Judge Parker let him off with a light sentence—one year in State Prison.[49]

The press decried the light sentence, which was apparently prompted by his advanced age and numerous petitions for clemency.[50]

Presumably, Morey returned to Calico after serving his sentence. He apparently remained there until 1897, when he sold the farm and homestead to Lewis Holman, who subsequently resold the property little more than a year later to Edward V. Brown. Brown sold the part of the property that lay north of the road to

Trees grow from the cellar hole of the Thomas Morey house not far from where Abel Broom was mortally wounded. *Courtesy of Rich Watson.*

Carmen Letner in 1900, but the remaining portion of the lot seems to have stayed in the Brown family until conveyed to George Thomas in 1921. By that time, the old Morey homestead was likely long gone.

George Ryan bought his first lot at Calico on the same day that Thomas Morey reacquired a small part of the enormous parcel. This 18.95 acre section began where the road to Tuckerton crosses Beaver Run. The following year, he purchased the lot situated between his home and the Morey farm. When writer Henry Beck visited the remains of the Ellis Adams farm in the 1930s, one of his escorts on the excursion claimed that George Mick had lived around the corner with the Ryan family.[51] Surprisingly, the scant vestiges of the Ryan home can still be located up the road to Warren Grove. Beck's informant recalled how Mick was known to steal pigs and horses from some of the neighbors from time to time. Perhaps he was fortunate to have never faced the consequences that befell poor Abel Broom! After George Ryan died, his heirs sold the 46.87 acre property back to the New Jersey Cranberry Company in 1888.[52]

There is some evidence to suggest that either the Ryan farmhouse or the homestead of Thomas Morey may have remained occupied into the 1900s. One of these structures seems to be mentioned in an article detailing a botanical expedition through the New Jersey Pine Barrens in 1899. C. F. Saunders and a group of botanists traveled from Philadelphia to Tuckerton, where they embarked on a 40 mile trek, which skirted the pine plains before turning west toward Atsion. The account details the party's findings throughout their journey, including the discovery of the elusive curly grass fern on the edge of a cedar swamp near Calico. The author then writes:

Not far from here we came upon the rarity of an inhabited house. There was an old stone-lined well in the shady yard, and as we leaned on the curbing while the bucket was bringing us up a drink, we were greeted with a beautiful sight of scores of fern plants clinging in the cool damp crevices of the stones far down in the well. *Phegopteris Dryopteris, Asplenium filixfoemina, Asplenium platyneuron*, and one of the varieties of *Dryopteris spinulosa* were collected. These are not at all Pine Barren species; indeed, *Phegopteris dryopteris* is a typical mountain form, and as far as New Jersey is concerned, *Britton's Catalogue* gives for it but two stations, both of which are in northern counties of the State, more than a hundred miles away. How it and its companions happened to get in that old well in the heart of the Pine Barrens is an interesting mystery.[53]

This out of the way house at Calico may well have been the old Thomas Morey farm. The catalpa-filled cellar hole beside Beaver Branch still betrays the site of the old homestead. Not long ago, some of the atypical ferns that Saunders identified in 1899, including a type of *Dryopteris spinulosa*, could still be found clinging to the remains of a stone-lined well at the site. The old water source that served the Morey family is merely a small depression today, but surprisingly, a few specimens of the *Asplenium platyneuron*, or Ebony Spleenwort, can still be found in the area. The wayward *Phegopteris dryopteris*, now referred to as *Gymnocarpium dryopteris* (L.) Newman, is more commonly called Oak Fern. Historian and botanist Ted Gordon confirms that this unusual visitor to the pines had vanished from Calico many years ago.[54]

Remains of the well mark the location of the George Ryan home site at Calico. The well that served the old farmhouse is mostly filled in by years of forest debris, but can still be located by those who know where to look for it. *Image courtesy of Rich Watson.*

Surprisingly some of the ferns discovered by Saunders more than a century ago could still be found at Calico when this picture of the Thomas Morey well was taken on August 21, 1982. Such wayward plants are occasionally found growing in the Pines where the land has been disturbed in the vicinity of old home sites. *Courtesy of Ted Gordon.*

THE THOMAS YEARS

Shortly after Samuel Dobbins Sr. died, George W. Thomas, from the neighboring village of Jenkins, became interested in the cranberry bogs at Calico. Thomas must have been well known in the area, as he served for a time as postmaster for the small settlement. For a period, he also sat on the Washington Township Board of Health, representing Jenkins Neck. On July 6, 1896, Samuel Dobbins Jr. acknowledged receipt of a check from Thomas for $150.00 "to be paid as per contract on cranberry bog."[55] The exact terms of this agreement are unknown, though it is possible that George Thomas began leasing the operation at this point in hopes of rejuvenating the surely neglected bogs. Perhaps this payment represented a first installment for the purchase of Dobbins' interest in the New Jersey Cranberry Company, though the transfer of his 120 shares to Thomas did not occur until August 1906.[56] Sometime during this ten-year period, various members of the Dobbins clan received half of Lippincott's remaining interest in the concern. Thomas and his family acquired many of these shares in 1908 and George's brother, Bertram, an attorney from Hainesport, succeeded in securing most of the other wayward shares in the company in the few years that followed.[57]

The water supply, so critical to the cultivation of cranberries, had always proven problematic at Calico, as the bogs there are set off from the Beaver Run stream that bypasses it to the south. The lengthy canal the original owners dug in the 1860s to flood the bogs was inadequate, if not a total failure. George Thomas soon developed plans for diverting water from a dam that backed up Beaver Run farther downstream in the vicinity of the old Thomas Morey homestead.[58] The route of this undertaking, likely started in 1909 or soon thereafter, can still be traced, especially where the shallow canal crosses the road to Warren Grove. Though it appears George Thomas made a considerable investment, the effort ultimately failed, presumably due to the inability to raise a high enough head of water at Beaver Run.

Forest fires, an insufficient water supply, and even trouble with the taxman challenged George Thomas in his cranberry-growing endeavor. Fortunately, in most years, the bogs produced a decent crop, and the income that Thomas obtained from cranberries supplemented his work as a carpenter. Later conveyances for the property indicate that Thomas would, on occasion, purchase property that abutted the bogs as the opportunities presented themselves.[59] It would appear that he finally solved some of the water problems at Calico by constructing a new canal that passed through the former lands of George Ryan to feed a reservoir above the cranberry meadows.

This source still serves as the main supply of water to the Calico bogs today.

In the spring of 1930, more than 60 forest fires raged through twelve counties in New Jersey. For more than three days, 35,000 men fought the conflagrations, which burned tens of thousands of acres. The pine belt was not spared, nor was the life of section fire warden George Thomas. On May 5, 1930, the Jenkins Neck resident succumbed to heat exhaustion while fighting the flames.[60] His remains rest in the Lower Bank cemetery.

This old sluice gate once controlled the flow of water from Beaver Branch to the cranberry bogs at Calico. Though the initial project proved to be a failure, George Thomas eventually succeeded in channeling water to his bogs by diverting the water through a different canal. *Courtesy of Richard Watson.*

CUTTS BROTHERS

On March 9, 1929, four brothers named Cutts purchased a 250 acre lot in Bass River Township from a man named Henry Silvert.[61] This parcel represented the western portion of one of the lots that Francis B. Chetwood created after he acquired the Martha Furnace Tract in 1859. The land they bought was just a stone's throw from where the paper mill at Harrisville had long prospered and was part of Lot 2 of Chetwood's so-called Oswego Lands. Soon, the four boys, who hailed from Tabernacle, would begin to acquire additional tracts in the area. Before long, Jack, Walter, Ross, and Ernest Cutts would begin to earn their livelihood growing berries in Bass River.

By the early 1930s, South Jersey witnessed the first extensive commercial cultivation of the blueberry. At their Bass River property near Calico, the Cutts began planting the newly improved varieties of blueberries that Frederick Coville and Elizabeth White had recently developed at Whitesbog near Pemberton. In short order, the four men had 100 acres of the fruit under cultivation.[62] Later, the family would expand their operations to Ivanhoe, North Carolina, to take advantage of the earlier growing season, and for a time, the partnership known as Cutts Brothers was the largest blueberry producer in the world.[63] Alongside their fields near Harrisville, the brothers built a sizable packing house to process blueberries and, later, cranberries. The Cutts also constructed a collection of cement-block picker shacks to create an extensive labor camp that became enlivened during the busy harvest season.[64]

The four brothers also knew something of the cranberry business, for their father John and his brothers had begun growing the tart fruit not far from the family home around 1900. These bogs were in the neighborhood of Goose Pond along the road from Tabernacle to Chatsworth. The vines that they set out were a variety known as Early Black, being the dominant berry in New Jersey at the time.[65]

In 1938, the Cutts purchased the Calico bogs from the heirs of George Thomas.[66] This cranberry plantation was but a small distance upstream from their own farm

and, in short order, the brothers improved and expanded these ancient bogs, first established in 1866. Subsequently, the family purchased the various tracts between these upper and lower bogs, creating a virtually contiguous parcel that included more than 7000 acres.[67]

As previously mentioned, when it comes to growing cranberries, the importance of an adequate fresh water supply cannot be overstated. In years past, overseers flooded the bogs to prevent damage from frost and insects. Now, "wet harvesting" in flooded bogs is the only practical method of bringing in the crop on today's modern plantations. As the Cutts Brothers acreage in Bass River grew, so too did their need for water.[68]

In the early 1960s, the brothers built a lift pump where one of their lots adjoined the Oswego stream, just a short distance above the former site of Martha Furnace. The pump itself consisted of a vertical shaft that drove a pair of impellers that lifted water from the river level through several compartments stacked atop one another. An excavated canal channeled the river water to the Calico bogs to supplement the flow of water to the main reservoir filled by diverting Beaver Run. Typically, the pump would need to run for several days before the ground along the canal became sufficiently saturated.[69] Though somewhat successful, the Cutts family eventually abandoned the pump, which quickly fell victim to vandalism. The old canal from the stream to the Calico bogs is easily traced, and the pump's carcass still sits in ruin beside the Oswego. Indeed, the vestiges of Cutts' pump is a favorite destination for local history enthusiasts.

By the early 1960s, the family made the decision to discontinue their blueberry business, and their many acres of cultivated bushes were allowed to become overgrown with brush. Today, the Pines have virtually reclaimed those fields.

By the 1970s, three of the brothers passed their interest in the company to Ernest and his two sons

Tickets like these were used by the Cutts family to keep track of the fruit picked by each worker during the busy harvest. *From the Richard Watson collection.*

Remnants of Cutts' pump in 2017. *Courtesy of Richard Watson.*

This photograph from the 1970s shows the lift pump on the Oswego that once supplied water to the Calico cranberry bogs. *Courtesy of Ted Gordon.*

(Ernest Jr. and Bill) who consolidated much of the family's land interests both in Bass River and Tabernacle.[70] Several years later, it seemed unlikely that anyone from the family would continue in the business, so the family sold much of their Bass River property, and eventually the State of New Jersey acquired most of the substantial tract.

The Cutts family continued to grow cranberries at Calico in what they call the "old bogs," and later developed acreage a short distance downstream. These lower bogs, appropriately enough, are called the "young bogs" by the family, and are not far from the blueberry fields they had established in the early 1930s. As fate would have it, later generations of Cutts did develop a passion for cranberry growing, and today, brothers Ernest and Bill, along with some of their children, work at Calico and other cranberry properties either full-time or during the busy harvest season.

Today, it is only periodic labors in the bogs and some curiosity about long vanished places that brings the occasional visitor to Calico. Nonetheless, the ancient site boasts a remarkable past. The venerable locale may have witnessed the glory days of iron in the pines. Calico also saw its way through the heady days of the "cranberry craze," and for a century and a half, rode that fickle industry through its long string of booms and busts. The small collection of homesteads that for decades sheltered hearty pioneers is long gone, having burned or rotted away more than a hundred years ago. Other than the extensive bogs, only a couple of cellar holes, scattered pieces of field stone and broken brick, along with an oyster shell or two, remain to mark the location of this long forgotten place.

ABOUT THE AUTHOR

Rich Watson grew up in the Taunton Lake section of Medford Township, Burlington County, where he developed a deep appreciation for the area's rich history. A graduate of Rutgers University, Rich has worked in the Lenape Regional High School District for the past 28 years, currently teaching Physics and Principles of Engineering at Seneca High School in Tabernacle. He has spent countless hours exploring the Pine Barrens and researching the region's former industries, its agriculture, and its long forgotten places. Rich is a member of the West Jersey History Roundtable. He and his family make their home in Tabernacle.

ENDNOTES

1 I. (Batchelder) James, "Mrs. T. P. James," *Memorial of Thomas Potts, Junior, Who Settled in Pennsylvania: with an Historic-Genealogical Account of His Descendants to the Eighth Generation* (Cambridge, MA: Privately printed, 1874).

2 John B. Smith, *The Insects Injuriously Affecting Cranberries*, New Jersey: Agricultural College Experiment Station, Special Bulletin K (1890): 3–4.

3 William H. Fischer, *Biographical Cyclopedia of Ocean County, New Jersey* (Philadelphia, PA: A. D. Smith Company, 1899), 74–77.

4 The Martha Furnace diary and daybook was reportedly discovered in the office of the Harrisville paper mill sometime prior to the 1910 fire that destroyed the factory there. Valued by historians for its unique insight into the operation of a Pine Barrens iron works, Henry H. Bisbee and his daughter Rebecca Bisbee Colesar transcribed the journal and published it in 1976 as *Martha: The Complete Martha Furnace Dairy and Journal 1808–1815*; see following note.

5 Henry H. Bisbee and Rebecca Bisbee Colesar, *Martha: The Complete Martha Furnace Diary and Journal 1808–1815* (Burlington, NJ: Henry Bisbee, Publisher, 1976).

6 Arthur D. Pierce, *Iron in the Pines: The Story of New Jersey's Ghost Towns and Bog Iron* (New Brunswick, NJ: Rutgers University Press, 1957) 84, 89.

7 William McMahon, *South Jersey Towns* (New Brunswick, NJ: Rutgers University Press, 1973), 129.

8 Barbara Solem-Stull, *Ghost Towns and Other Quirky Places in the New Jersey Pine Barrens* (Medford, NJ: Plexus Publishing, Inc. 2005), 112.

9 J. W. Otley, and R. Whiteford, *Map of Burlington County Mostly from Original Surveys* (Philadelphia: Smith & Wister, 1849).

10 C. Shimer Boyer, *Early Forges & Furnaces in New Jersey* (Philadelphia: University of Pennsylvania Press, 1963), 114.

11 Burlington County Clerk [Deed] Book Q3, 47.

12 Burlington County Clerk [Deed] Book X3, 259.

13 Burlington County Clerk [Deed] Book X3, 260.

14 Burlington County Clerk [Deed] Book X3, 261.

15 "Fire in the Pines," *Commercial Advertiser* (New York, NY), August 11, 1838, 2.

16 Pierce, *Iron in the Pines*, 16, 92.

17 Boyer, *Early Forges & Furnaces in New Jersey*, 119.

18 "Improvement in New Jersey," *Centinel of Freedom* (Newark, NJ), July 10, 1855, 3.

19 Burlington County Clerk [Deed] Book K4, 468.

20 Henry Charlton Beck, *Forgotten Towns of Southern New Jersey* (New Brunswick, NJ: Rutgers University Press, 1961), 85–87.

21 Burlington County Clerk [Deed] Book N7, 95.

22 Burlington County Clerk [Deed] Book Q5, 154.

23 Burlington County Clerk [Deed] Book W5, 34.

24 *New Jersey Mirror* (Mount Holly, NJ), June 21, 1855.

25 Burlington County Clerk [Deed] W5, 34.

26 Burlington County Clerk [Deed] V5, 125.

27 Samuel S. Downs, *Map of Oswego Lands Formerly Martha Survey* (Tuckerton NJ, 1859).

28 *New Jersey Biographical Dictionary*, 2nd ed. (St. Clair Shores, MI: Somerset Publishers, Inc., 1999).

29 "The Working Farmer 12," *Cranberry Lands* (New York, NY: Charles V. Mapes, 1860), 5.

30 Burlington County Clerk [Deed] A8, 578.

31 Burlington County Surrogate [Will] Book K, 435.

32 Burlington County Clerk [Deed] Book K7, 377.

33 Burlington County Clerk [Certificate of Incorporation] Book A of Corporations, 237.

34 New Jersey Cranberry Company records [stock transfer book]. Richard Watson collection.

35 Burlington County Clerk [Deed] Book U7, 16.

36 S. B. Phinney, *Cranberry Culture*, Report of the United States Department of Agriculture (Washington: Government Printing Office), 1863, 131.

37 New Jersey Cranberry Company records [stock transfer book]. Richard Watson collection.

38 New Jersey Cranberry Company records [bank book]. Richard Watson collection.

39 Burlington County Clerk [Deed] Book K7, 386.

40 Burlington County Clerk [Deed] Book 289, 431.

41 Burlington County Clerk [Deed] Book K7, 388.

42 Burlington County Clerk [Deed] Book S7, 261.

43 Burlington County Clerk [Deed] Book V8, 203.

44 Burlington County Clerk [Deed] Book V8, 205.

45 Beck, *Forgotten Towns of Southern New Jersey*, 85–87.

46 "Shooting of a Truck Thief," *Philadelphia Inquirer*, August 27, 1887.

47 "One Year in Prison for Murder," *New York Herald-Tribune*, November 11, 1887.

48 "Pleaded Guilty," *Philadelphia Inquirer*, October 25, 1887.

49 "Throughout the State," *Trenton Evening Times* (Trenton, NJ) November 17, 1887.

50 "One Year in Prison for Murder," *New York Herald-Tribune*, November 11, 1887.

51 Beck, *Forgotten Towns of Southern New Jersey*, 85–87.

52 Burlington County Clerk [Deed] Book W11, 627.

53 C. F. Saunders, "The Pine Barrens of New Jersey," *Proceedings of the Academy of Natural Sciences* 52 (1900).

54 Ted Gordon, Interview, September 21, 2017.

55 New Jersey Cranberry Company records [receipt]. Richard Watson collection.

56 New Jersey Cranberry Company records [stock transfer book]. Richard Watson collection.

57 New Jersey Cranberry Company records [George Thomas Correspondence]. Richard Watson collection.

58 New Jersey Cranberry Company records [map of plan for flooding bogs at Calico]. Richard Watson collection.

59 Burlington County Clerk [Deed] Book 1832, 57.

60 *The Scranton Republican* (Scranton, PA), May 6, 1930, 1.

61 Burlington County Clerk [Deed] Book 731, 370.

62 "Cutts Brothers of New Jersey, Sound Operators," *Cranberries, The National Cranberry Magazine* 18, no. 9 (January 1954): 10.

63 Ernest Cutts, Bill Cutts and Dan Cutts, Interview, September 15, 2017.

64 Ibid.

65 "Cutts Brothers of New Jersey, Sound Operators," *Cranberries, The National Cranberry Magazine* 18, no. 9 (January 1954): 10.

66 Burlington County Clerk [Deed] Book 896, 120.

67 Burlington County Clerk [Deed] Book 1832, 57.

68 "Cutts Brothers of New Jersey, Sound Operators," *Cranberries, The National Cranberry Magazine* 18, no. 9 (January 1954).

69 Ernest Cutts, Bill Cutts and Dan Cutts, Interview, September 15, 2017.

70 Ibid.

Crabbe family bogs at Double Trouble. Although not a view of the cranberry bogs at Calico, these bogs were similar. This rare postcard image depicts a group of fieldworkers engaged in dry picking cranberries on a warm sunny day, as attested by the woman with a bonnet on the right, who is depositing her pickings in the woven basket in front of her. Someone with the initials of J. R. T. mailed this card on June 20, 1909, to Mrs. J. B. Lowe in Passaic, New Jersey, and indicated that he would be involved in such cranberry picking in the fall.

Plagues and Public Policy:
How South Jersey Cleaned Up Its Act

Claude Epstein

People often complain about governmental interference with their individual rights. Yet, in some cases, they have sought governmental intervention to solve problems beyond their personal control. Such is the case of infectious diseases. This article will summarize South Jersey's experience, over time, of providing clean, potable water and developing sewage treatment, with a focus on waterborne diseases, specifically cholera, typhoid fever, and poliomyelitis, which generated a great deal of fear among the New Jersey public.

HISTORICAL CONTEXT

For eons prior to the nineteenth century, virtually all people held the responsibility for providing their own supply of household water and energy and handling the disposal of personal sewage. Most carried a bucket to obtain their water, usually from a pond, spring, river, or shallow-dug well, and then lugged it back to their homes. Some had cisterns in basements or nearby locations, which they filled with water from another source. No power companies then existed, resulting in people acquiring oil and firewood or coal to create their own energy for lighting, heating, and cooking. Likewise, government had yet to form any sewerage authorities. Each home had a privy (i.e., outhouse) with an underlying vault, where human wastes accumulated. These vaults required emptying periodically and the waste disposed of elsewhere. Regretfully, a total lack of sanitary landfills led to people piling up their extraneous rubbish and waste at some location out of sight. In addition, many people on farms and proximate to towns lived close to their barnyards, exposing them to livestock waste as well as their own (Figure 1).

Living in the twenty-first century, very few of us have grown up with livestock. In previous times, at least until the early twentieth century, many people lived much closer to farm animals. In earliest colonial times, livestock roamed freely through towns, woodlands, and meadows for grazing (Figure 2). Early colonial laws merely regulated the penning of animals as a preventative for property destruction. No one even considered the hazards livestock presented to human health, so lawmakers passed no laws regulating these public health issues.

Prior to *en masse* motorized vehicle sales in the early twentieth century, horses provided the primary motive power for personal transportation, accompanying people in most of their daily activities,

Figure 1. Human and livestock waste accumulation in a typical barnyard.[1]

as shown in Figure 3. Horses traveled throughout the roadways of South Jersey, either ridden or pulling wagons, carts, carriages, and stagecoaches. South Jersey farms employed draft horses for all sorts of chores. The odor

Figure 2. Cows roaming the countryside, Hurffville, c. 1907. *Courtesy of the Paul W. Schopp collection.*

County	1726[2]	1810[3]	2010[3]
Atlantic			494
Burlington	5	30	562
Camden			2322
Cape May	3	16	387
Cumberland		26	324
Gloucester (incl. Atlantic & Camden until 1837 and 1844, respectively)	2	20	895
Monmouth (incl. Ocean until 1850)	5	21	1345
Ocean			917
Salem	5	42	288

Table 1. Population density of South Jersey counties (people/mi²).

from manure in town and on the farm provided a common olfactory experience. The accumulation of livestock waste in manure piles and elsewhere, like human waste, required continual removal. This eventually led to the waste disposal industry. Manure proved useful as a farmfield or garden fertilizer and as a raw material for various chemical manufactories. But aside from its noxious odor, few considered it a danger to public health.

SOUTH JERSEY POPULATION GROWTH

South Jersey's non-indigenous population grew progressively from its first European settlements. The people residing in South Jersey numbered in the low hundreds before the Quakers from Great Britain arrived and initially formed the communities of Salem and Burlington. The population soon increased into the thousands. Of course, original population densities began low, but grew exponentially over the decades (Table 1). And as people dwelled in ever-closer proximity, the probability of infecting one another proportionally increased.

Under constitutional requirement, the federal government began taking a decennial census in 1790. The population of each South Jersey county grew slowly from then to the 1880s. But the growth rate accelerated markedly after 1880, due largely to immigration (Figure 4).[4] Per capita water consumption was likewise initially low, but expanded with population growth.

THE PLAGUES OF SOUTH JERSEY

Prior to the nineteenth century, people had little understanding of what caused disease. Some believed that a deity introduced maladies as punishment for transgressions or that diseases were due to malevolent curses. This began to change in ancient Greece with the birth of medicine. But alternative understandings of infectious disease had to wait numerous centuries.

By the end of the eighteenth century, the perceived spiritual causes of disease had yielded to an environ-

mental explanation with the development of the miasma theory. This model suggested that bad air, a miasma emanating from rotting organic matter in town trash piles and stagnant swamps, generated disease. By the end of the nineteenth century, germ theory had replaced miasma theory. Researchers recognized microbes and correlated them with specific infectious diseases which, as a result, led to treatments for these diseases.[5]

Whatever the cause, epidemics were, and still are, a fact of life. These outbreaks swept large numbers of people from the earth, generating widespread fear. What was the cause? Closer to home, New Jersey and neighboring colonies endured repeated outbreaks of infectious diseases.[6] Small pox, yellow fever, measles, cholera, typhoid fever and, later, polio ravaged the region. The earliest personal protection involved leaving towns or quarantining the sick.

Control of infectious diseases occurred in two steps, even before the medical world fully understood the mechanics of such maladies. The Sanitary Movement, born out of the massive mortalities of the Civil

Figure 3. Downtown Burlington, c.1907. *Courtesy of the Paul W. Schopp collection.*

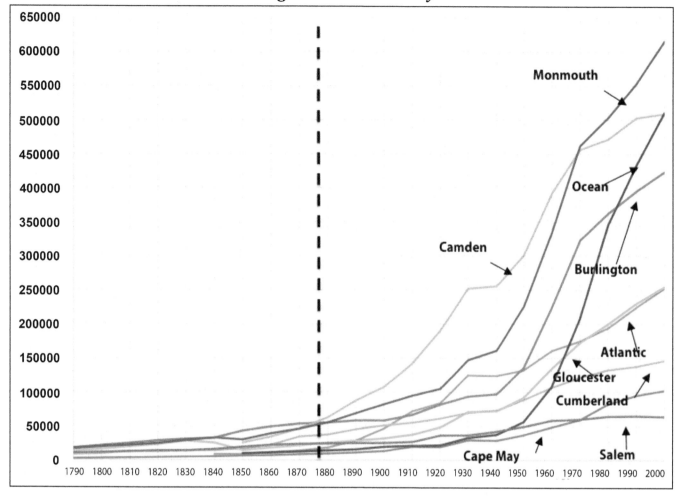

Figure 4. Population of South Jersey counties.

War and similar conflicts in Europe during the middle and late nineteenth century, stressed epidemiology and cleanliness. Water quality, food supply contamination, as well as the disposal of sewage and other wastes, were among the Sanitarians main concerns. They believed that disease originated with the accumulation of human wastes in and near settlements or nearby stagnant water and swampy conditions. The movement of infection from one individual to another, however, was discounted.

As a result of failing to observe the personal infectious nature of diseases, many fathers, mothers, sons, and daughters died of such illnesses in the nineteenth century; it was simply a fact of everyday life. The wealthy, the powerful, but especially the poor were vulnerable. Cities grew and outbreaks became more virulent and frequent. As noted in the previous paragraph, war brought death to many combatants due to the squalor of camp life. Anxiety over these conditions required a solution. The accumulation of filth and the nearness of fetid wetlands were blamed. It was not till the end of the nineteenth century that most physicians accepted germ theory and recognized the microbial cause of disease.

The second step of infectious disease control involved the development of germ theory in the latter part of the nineteenth century. This theory cited microorganisms as the cause of disease and asserted that infection spread between individuals. While Anton van Leeuwenhoek had invented the microscope and described the first microorganisms in 1683, it took almost two hundred years for the first correlation of microbes and diseases to take place. In 1873, Gerhard Hansen was the first to recognize this correlation with leprosy, where the bacterium *Myciobacterium leprosae* was the cause. Three years later, Robert Koch demonstrated that the anthrax bacterium caused anthrax, a disease that affected cattle.[7] Soon, other specific microorganisms were identified as the causes of many other diseases.

WATERBORNE DISEASES

Cholera, typhoid fever, and poliomyelitis are among the waterborne diseases that brought fear and loathing to New Jersey citizens. Cholera and typhoid fever originate with the bacterium *Vibrio cholera* (identified in 1883) and *Eberthella typhi* (identified in 1884), respectively.[8] Polio enters the body from a virus, first identified in 1908.[9]

These late nineteenth-century studies confirmed the relationship between many infectious diseases and water contaminated with infected fecal matter.

Cholera

The earliest epidemics to strike the New Jersey area, smallpox and yellow fever, were on the wane when cholera first appeared in New Jersey in 1832.[10] Cholera was a terrifying disease to those living in nineteenth-century America. It was known to have claimed hundreds and thousands of victims in India, its place of origin. In the late 1820s, a new epidemic passed out of India, made its way across Asia to Europe, and finally arrived in Britain by 1831.[11] It was only a matter of months before it struck the east coast cities of America. Table 2 shows which cities, in and near New Jersey, developed cases of cholera. New York and Philadelphia were major ports of entry. The disease came to the east coast via passengers and crew and then spread from there to the surrounding regions. Dates assigned to these epidemics vary from author to author. Those depicted below are generally from the earliest published sources. A small number of cholera cases still occur in New Jersey, but they are rare and seldom fatal.

Typhoid Fever

Typhoid fever existed in South Jersey throughout the eighteenth and nineteen centuries, but cases and mortality were not accurately recorded until 1880. In that year, the New Jersey State Legislature passed "an act concerning the protection of the public health and the record of vital facts and statistics relating thereto."[19] Three years earlier, they had established the State Board of Health,

but the 1880 act went further.[20] It established the Bureau of Vital Statistics that tracked not only births, marriages, and deaths, but also causes of death, and statistics on immigration and professions. In addition, this act established local boards of health that reported on the public health of each municipality in the state. As a consequence, the temporal and geographical distribution of diseases became far more accurately recorded after 1880. As it turned out, typhoid fever was the twelfth largest cause of death in New Jersey between 1879 and 1900, just after cancer.[21]

Cholera had ceased to be much of a concern by the turn of the twentieth century, with typhoid becoming the major waterborne disease. Figure 5 shows the distribution of typhoid fever in the nine South Jersey Counties from 1912 through 1961.[18, 22] Burlington, Camden and Monmouth counties had more cases of typhoid than the other counties. The overall trend was on a downward trajectory as typhoid fever outbreaks became far less serious after 1938. The reason for this dramatic decline can be linked to the development of safer water supplies.

Case Study: Pitman Grove[23]

Pitman Grove in Mantua Township, Gloucester County, began as a seasonal Methodist camp meeting in 1871, where revival meetings were held in the summer months. This location serves as a perfect exemplar for typical contamination issues, and the potential for a cholera or typhoid outbreak, prior to governmental oversight. The camp meeting grounds consisted of 600 cottages for its attendees set close together and separated by narrow streets. Its population typically ranged from between 5000 and 7000 people but could reach 15000

Table 2. Jersey Epidemics					
Epidemic of 1832[12]			**Epidemic of 1849**[13, 14]		
Location	*Date*	*Year*	New York	2-Dec	1848
New York	26-Jun	1832	Philadelphia	22-May	1849
Philadelphia	5-Jul	1832	Newark	4-Jun	1849
Chatham	14-Jul	1832	Paterson	6-Jun	1849
Newark	7-Jul	1832	**Epidemic of 1854**[15, 16]		
New Brunswick	14-Jul	1832	New York	29-May	1854
Elizabethtown	14-Jul	1832	Philadelphia	17-Jun	1854
Trenton	14-Jul	1832	Newark	June	1854
Paterson	14-Jul	1832	**Epidemic of 1865–66**[17]		
Princeton	14-Jul	1832	New York	18-Apr	1865
Burlington	14-Jul	1832	**Epidemic of 1873**[18]		
Camden	14-Jul	1832	New York	12-Nov	1873
Jersey City	26-Jul	1832	Philadelphia	21-Jun	1873

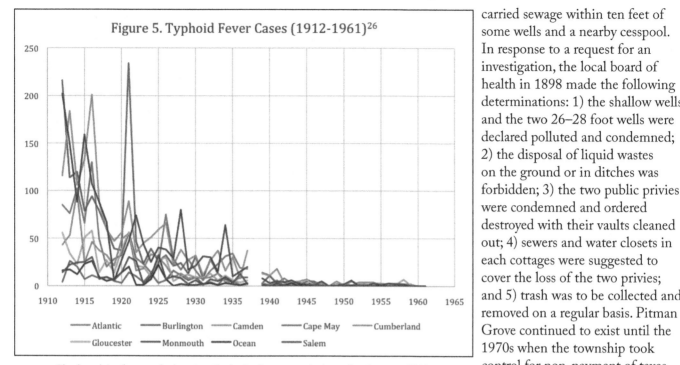

The break in the graph denotes the lack of an annual report for the year 1938.

carried sewage within ten feet of some wells and a nearby cesspool. In response to a request for an investigation, the local board of health in 1898 made the following determinations: 1) the shallow wells and the two 26–28 foot wells were declared polluted and condemned; 2) the disposal of liquid wastes on the ground or in ditches was forbidden; 3) the two public privies were condemned and ordered destroyed with their vaults cleaned out; 4) sewers and water closets in each cottages were suggested to cover the loss of the two privies; and 5) trash was to be collected and removed on a regular basis. Pitman Grove continued to exist until the 1970s when the township took control for non-payment of taxes.

during camp meeting activities (Figure 6). Its water supply consisted of 1) a well, drilled to 180 feet below grade, which connected to only 30 of the community buildings; 2) two wells, set 26 to 28 feet below the surface, whose water was sold to Philadelphia restaurants; and 3) many tube wells, set only 15 to 18 feet below the surface, which supplied most of the attendees with potable water. Its bathroom facilities consisted of two large privies that served most of the camp. The surface soil did not drain well, so that dishwater, emptied outside the cottages on the ground, formed pools in the roadways. Trash storage on the ground accumulated in piles or in boxes. As would be expected, Pitman Grove became unhealthy. Its two privies received too much use, overflowed, and created a noxious odor. In addition, a shallow ditch on the grounds

Figure 6. Pitman Grove (Mantua Township, Gloucester County) in 1907. *Courtesy of the Paul W. Schopp collection.*

POLIOMYELITIS

A small number of polio outbreaks occurred in nineteenth-century America, though not in New Jersey. In 1910, polio was added to the list of diseases the Bureau of Vital Statistics monitored. The bureau recorded 102 individual cases in 35 different localities, but this was nothing like future outbreaks.[24] Polio, unlike the other two mentioned waterborne diseases, derived from a virus, not a bacterium, though all three bred in water contaminated with fecal matter. The Bureau of Vital Statistics reported on cases and deaths due to polio in its records from 1912 forward.

Figure 7 shows the distribution of polio cases from 1912 to 1961.[25] The overall pattern was distinct from that of typhoid fever. While typhoid occurred in numerous serious outbreaks prior to the 1930s, the number of cases greatly declined after 1938. From then on, typhoid fever occurred in minor outbreaks, almost disappearing. Polio, with the exception of the polio outbreak of 1916, only reached the number of cases experienced with typhoid in the early twentieth century after the 1930s. The major outbreaks occurred in 1916, 1939, and 1949. Moderate outbreaks occurred in 1932, 1945, 1952, and 1954. In addition, more cases of polio occurred after 1938 than before. It is almost as if polio replaced typhoid fever as the most powerful waterborne scourge. But from 1961 on, polio ceased to be much of a concern as the Salk and Sabin vaccines had put an end to it for the most part.

The outbreaks of these three diseases, especially cholera and typhoid fever, stimulated the activities of the New

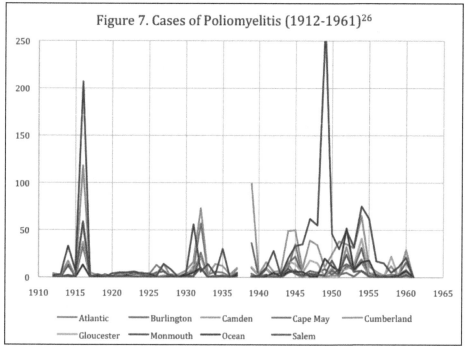

Figure 7. Cases of Poliomyelitis (1912-1961)[26]

Atlantic — Burlington — Camden — Cape May — Cumberland
Gloucester — Monmouth — Ocean — Salem

The break in the graph denotes the lack of an annual report for the year 1938.

THE SANITARIAN MOVEMENT AND THE CREATION OF THE STATE BOARD OF HEALTH

David Cowen has described the Sanitarian Movement in New Jersey.[27] The New Jersey Medical Society set up a committee to look into developing a legal framework to insure public health in 1849. They determined that existing laws were inadequate in 1853. Dr. Ezra M. Hunt, an important figure in creation of New Jersey public health awareness and institutional development, formulated a *programme* before the medical societies and the governor of the State in 1866. He said that charity was inadequate to deal with these issues of public health and that the government had to step in to establish and enforce rules to protect public health; it also needed to begin educating the state's population on safeguarding their health. People did not undergo all the expense and disruption in their lives to develop clean water supplies and safe waste disposal just because it was a good idea. Fear of disease was a major impetus. People needed some explanation for the causes of diseases.

The state legislature established the New Jersey Sanitary Association in 1875 and the New Jersey Board of Health two years later. Finally, in 1880 state lawmakers empowered the State Board of Health with enforcement authority, and enabled the development of local boards of health for each municipality in the state. The legislators also established the Bureau of Vital Statistics to keep track of births, deaths, diseases, and other parameters.

The New Jersey Board of Health prepared a questionnaire that, for each local board of health, had to be submitted annually. It covered twenty-three factors needed to safeguard the public's health.[28] The State had now taken over what had been a private matter.

TYPHOID CONTAMINATION OF THE FOOD SUPPLY

The typhoid fever threat was not only found in the water supply. Personnel working in various sectors of the food-supply chain could also pose a hazard. The State Board of Health looked into typhoid infections from farms, creameries, ice cream manufactories, icehouses, and shellfisheries. Employees were capable of passing the infection, even though they might be symptom free. The most notorious case of this was Mary Mallon, known as Typhoid Mary.[29] She worked as a cook for several

Jersey Sanitarian movement and the State legislature. The water supply, then the disposal of sewage, became the focus of their activities, regulations, and technologies developed to meet the challenge.

EARLY NINETEENTH-CENTURY WATER SUPPLY AND SEWAGE TREATMENT

Public health concerns in South Jersey were not just a problem of congested cities, but of rural areas as well. As mentioned previously, water supply and waste disposal was an individual's concern, not the responsibility of the government. Early per capita water consumption was far lower than it is today. One way to look at early and present water consumption is to compare modern developed and undeveloped countries.[26]

	Consumption	Domestic	Industrial	Agriculture
	m³/person/year	% per capita	% per capita	% per capita
United States	2162	12	40	42
Canada	1752	11	80	8
India	612	3	4	93
Chad	35	16	2	82

Table 3. Modern per capita water consumption.[27]

As one would expect, developed countries have the highest consumption per person. Water use for domestic purposes is relatively low for all countries presented while agricultural use is greatest in the undeveloped countries.

Location, population, climate	markets	cemeteries, burials
geology, topography, contour	animal diseases	public health laws & regulations
water-supply	slaughter houses & abattoirs	registration & vital statistics
drainage, sewerage	manufactories & trade	quarantine, care & vaccination
streets, public grounds	schools, public buildings	sanitary expenses
houses & tenancy	almshouses, hospitals, charities	building's heat & ventilation
modes of lighting	police, prisons	report on health conditions
refuse & excreta management	fire guards	

Table 4. Items reviewed by local boards of health.[29]

wealthy New York families, who mysteriously came down with typhoid fever.

At about the same time, the New Jersey Board of Health began to investigate the contamination of the food supply. The local boards in Bordentown and Chesterfield visited several farms to observe their sanitary conditions, which provides an opportunity to describe the then existing problems. Nineteenth- and early twentieth-century farmers raising cows, sheep, swine, poultry, and goats not only had to provide their livestock's water needs, but also handle the subsequent waste removal. Even farmers that only grew vegetables and cereal crops required horses to perform farm tasks. Table 5 illustrates that farmers had a separate source for livestock water and waste disposal. The proximity of barns and manure piles to the livestock water supply, as well as the proximity of the privy to the farmstead's water supply, could lead to unhealthy conditions.

For example, workers, using draft horses, cut ice from ponds in winter and stored the large frozen blocks in icehouses. Ice companies then sold the product in warmer seasons to prevent food spoilage. An inspection found ice in Asbury Park contaminated with sewage, which led to a state study and a law prohibiting polluting ice ponds in 1885.[30]

The Board of Health soon scrutinized dairy products and identified contaminated milk as the cause of typhoid outbreaks in Montclair and Bayhead during 1894,[31] which led to the inspection of dairies beginning in the same year.[32] Legislation gained approval to register milk cows and inspect their living conditions in 1896.[33] In 1910, another law passed forbidding the use of milk cows and dairy utensils washed with contaminated water.[34] Dairy products blended in creameries began being inspected during 1906.[35] Prohibition of the sale of

Farmer's Name	Source (for livestock)	Well Depth (ft)	Distance from Stable (ft)	Distance From Manure Pile (ft)	Source (house)	Well Depth (ft)	Distance from Privy (ft)	Distance to Open Drain
J. L. Klein	Well		40	20	Well		40	
Jos. DeCou	Well	20	20	20	Well (under kitchen)	50	65	
Benj. Holloway	Well	16	20	5		15	50	near
J. H. Colkitt	Same	15			Well (under kitchen)	15	150	
E. P. Newell	Spring				Well (under house)	22	48	27
E. P. Newell	Brook							
Wm. Allen	Public				Public			
D. C. Coleman	Well		30		Well (under house)	36	39	
Frank Applegate	Well		30	5	Well (under house)	21	84	5
H. F. Satterthwaite	Well		50	40	Well (under kitchen)	30	50	15

Table 5. Parameters measured on farm visits by board of health.[37]

all dairy products handled by workers thought to have communicable diseases passed in 1910, expanding a 1898 law that only applied to milk.[36] Inspection of ice creameries also began at this time as well.

The Board also turned its focus on the shellfish industry. The State passed a law in 1887 forbidding the sale of unwholesome oysters and clams. The State approved another act charging the Board of Health with the responsibility for inspecting clam and oyster beds annually, thereby ascertaining their sanitary condition. This law also granted the Board the authority to condemn the use of unsanitary beds and the sale of clams and oysters from beds considered unsanitary.[38] A clam-related typhoid outbreak occurred in Lumberton during 1911.[39] Ocean City also suffered a rather serious outbreak in the same year.[40] Typhoid broke out in four hotels during the summer tourist season. This outbreak traced back to clams taken from the Thorofare behind Ocean City, where a hospital treating typhoid patients dumped its sewage. At least 30 people were stricken. Now typhoid outbreaks were more than a danger to public health. They were also a threat to the shore economy.

The Development of Safe Water Supplies

The fear of typhoid outbreaks and the scare of cholera led the State Board of Health to secure New Jersey's water supplies. Now, control of water supply and sewage disposal passed from individuals into State hands. The state board required each township to develop a public water supply, which could be township owned or leased to private companies.

Several South Jersey communities had already established a public water supply prior to the creation of the State Board of Health. Some of the larger communities in the Delaware Valley instituted the earliest public water supplies. These include Burlington (1804), Mount Holly (1846), Camden (1853), and Bordentown (1856). Bridgeton and Millville founded theirs in 1876 and 1878 respectively. The resort towns of Cape May City (1874), Cape May Point (1876), and Long Branch (1877) initiated water supplies for their citizens and tourists. But the bulk of public water supplies became a reality following the formation of the State Board (Table 6).[41] Groundwater proved to be the major source of supply once well drillers developed the technology to reach deeper aquifers in the 1890s.[42] The drilling of artesian wells, safe from surface contamination, provided clean water to 22 South Jersey communities by 1908. Surficial water, obtained from streams, supplied 23 South Jersey communities with a sufficient water supply. These population centers derived domestic water from the Delaware River, as well as the Rancocas Creek, Mantua

Creek, Metedeconk Creek, and other smaller streams. A few towns utilized springs and lakes. Finally, Monmouth Beach, Sea Bright, and Palmyra had their water piped in from other communities.

Municipal water supply systems comprised more than just the water's source. Pipes carried the water from the source to a collection site, either a reservoir or a large storage tank. From these storage facilities, water mains, at first made of wood and then of iron, distributed the water throughout the district being supplied, delivering it to individual homes and businesses. By the turn of the twentieth century, the New Jersey Board of Health provided a yearly accounting of water main extensions and the number of homes connected in their annual reports.[43]

Once houses and businesses received running water, a whole host of conveniences could become widespread. Initially, only the wealthy few had such luxuries. The White House received "running water" beginning in 1833 during Franklin Pierce's administration. With running water installed, people could bathe and wash laundry at a greater frequency. A major invention was the water closet (i.e., flush toilet). While the first prototype was invented in 1775, the modern flush toilet was only developed in 1891. Flowing water now served to remove human waste from the home.[44]

The Development of Sewage Treatment Facilities

The now safe municipal water supplies flowing into homes and businesses increased overall per capita consumption. This, in turn, gave rise to a new problem—wastewater disposal. Privy vaults, cesspools, and local sewers soon became overwhelmed. Immediately following the municipal takeover of the water supply, local governments responded to the need for wastewater disposal. Those sewerage systems that already existed only handled surface runoff removal, but they could also be used for wastewater removal. By the turn of the twentieth century, municipalities constructed sewer lines to accommodate safe removal of effluent (Table 7).

Within a short time, most houses and businesses featured municipal main connections. But this merely collected the wastewater and dumped it untreated into the rivers, bays, and coastal waters of South Jersey. It soon became apparent that this situation was untenable. When typhoid fever passed through seafood, it placed at risk the tourism sector of the economy and the active shellfisheries along the Jersey shore and bayshore.[47] Floating wastes discharged from treatment plant outfalls created unsightly and offensive nuisances along the beaches.[48] Various municipal water supplies in the

Location	Date	Supply	Location	Date	Supply
			Maple Shade	1894	
Allenhurst	1896	Artesian Wells	Matawan		
Asbury Park	1886	Artesian Wells	Medford	1895	Creek
Atlantic City	1883	Art. Wells, Stream	Merchantville	1897	Stream
Atlantic Highlands	1893	Artesian Wells	Millville	1878	Wells
Avalon	1898	Artesian Wells	Monmouth Beach	1887	from Long Branch
Bay Head	1889	Artesian Wells	Moorestown	1888	Springs
Beach Haven	1893	Artesian Wells	Mount Holly	1846	Rancocas Cr.
Belmar	1897	Artesian Wells	Neptune City		
Beverly	1887	Delaware River	Ocean City	1893	Artesian Wells
Bordentown	1856	Delaware R., Wells	Ocean Grove	1884	
Bridgeton	1876	Springs	Palmyra		Riverton Well
Burlington	1804	Delaware River	Pemberton	1894	Wells
Camden	1853	Artesian Wells	Pitman Grove	1901	Driven Wells
Cape May City	1874	Dug Well	Red Bank	1885	Artesian Wells
Cape May C. H.	1895	Driven Wells	Riverside		Delaware River
Cape May Point	1876	Artesian Wells	Riverton	1889	Wells
Clayton	1895	Driven Wells	Salem	1882	Artesian Wells
Collingswood	1891	Springs	Sea Bright	1882	from Long Branch
Darlington	1895	Artesian Wells	Sea Isle City	1895	Artesian Wells
Deal	1887	Brooks	Shrewsbury	1882	Brooks
Eatontown			Spring Lake		
Egg Harbor City	1896	Artesian Wells	Swedesboro	1901	Wells
Freehold	1891	Artesian Wells	Toms River		
Glassboro	1896	Driven Wells	Tuckerton	1898	Lake
Gloucester City	1884	Springs, Creek	Vincentown	1896	Rancocas Cr.
Haddonfield	1886	Stream	Vineland	1886	Driven Wells
Hammonton	1903	Artesian Wells	Wenonah	1885	Springs
Highlands	1886	Springs	West Cape May		
Keyport	1893	Artesian Wells	Woodlynne	1901	Camden wells
Lakewood	1886	Metedeconk R.	Wildwood		Artesian Wells
Long Branch	1877	Brooks	Woodbury	1886	Mantua Creek
Longport	1895	Artesian Wells	Woodstown	1892	Artesian Wells

Table 6. Opening date of South Jersey public water supplies.[45, 46]

Delaware and Raritan Valleys suffered contamination from discharged wastewater.[49] Finally, wastewater discharge created local nuisances for people and industries near treatment plant outfalls.[50] The wastewater would need to be "treated" to reduce the risk of waterborne disease, economic loss, and local nuisances.

The major means of purifying wastewater at the treatment plant involved screening, sedimentation, filtration, application onto land surfaces, and disinfection.[51] The wastewater initially underwent "pretreatment" in the form of screening. It passed through a coarse screen when entering the treatment plant, removing the solid debris from the wastewater, such as branches, rags, pieces of lumber, bottles, etc. Sedimentation involved collecting the wastewater in a large tank so that solid particles could fall to the bottom by gravitational settling and greases, oils, and waxes could rise to the surface. The next steps employed biological processes. Bacteria, algae, fungi, and protozoa grown on various kinds of solid surfaces formed a biomass or slime layer that digested organic matter from the wastewater. The various methods used for this biological filtration included contact

Location	Length	Location	Length	Location	Length
Allenhurst	4	Camden	52	N. Spring Lake	6
Asbury Park	*	Collingswood	6.5	Ocean City	5
Atlantic City	30	Deal	7	Ocean Grove	7
Avalon	2.8	Freehold	7	Pemberton	1.25
Beach Haven	2.5	Haddonfield	14	Red Bank	9
Belmar	12	Lakewood	9	Riverton	1.0
Bordentown	**	Long Branch	8	Salem	3
Burlington	10	Longport	0.5	Swedesboro	1.5

Table 7. Lengths (miles) of municipal sewage pipes by 1902.[46] *All mains constructed; ** Three mains constructed.

beds, trickling filters, sprinkling filters, and sand filters, removing about 90 percent of the organic matter. By the mid-1950s, a typical sewage treatment plant had the following processing components:

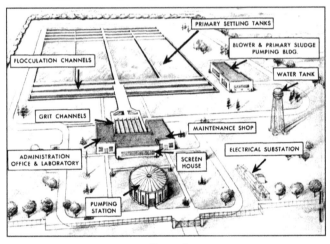

Figure 8.

In some locations, an additional process existed, the application of sewage on land surfaces. Surface application used natural soil or ecological processes to remove nutrients from the applied sewage. Surface applications included land filtration, sand seepage, broad irrigation, subsurface filtration, and diversion to seepage ditches. Finally, one technique used was disinfection. Here the sewage was exposed to chlorine or calcium hypochlorite, and, in a single case, copper sulfate. This would dissolve organic matter and eliminate bacteria.

By 1910, 82 treatment plants were in operation and another twelve under construction (Table 8).[52] From then until now, municipalities and sewerage authorities added or improved many more treatment plants. Today, the number of discharge permits the New Jersey Department of Environmental Protection issues establishes the aggregate of sewerage and wastewater treatment plants operating in the state, amounting to 853 facilities.[53] The scope of wastewater treatment operations has expanded (Table 9). Some are meant for specific activities like dentists' offices and medical wastes, water coolants for

machinery, and the disposal of concrete product. Additional filters and disinfectants have been added to the treatment-plant arsenal. The solids, or residues, that accumulate in sedimentation tanks and other treatment collectors receive more attention. In the past, these solids would be transported and disposed of in landfills. Now, the volume is severely reduced through moisture removal processes in drying basins, lined impoundments, and freshwater wetlands (e.g., reed beds). The dewatered residues can then be applied to land surfaces, incinerated, stored in transfer stations or disposed of in landfills. Liquid wastes can also be disposed of on land surfaces by irrigation or placed beneath the land surface in subsurface collectors (i.e., large collection basins) and passed on into the soil or into a convenient body of water, or even injected into the groundwater. Moreover, modern technology has developed treatment plants to handle petroleum product spills and site remediation clean ups.

Subsequent to the initial construction of sewage treatment plants at the onset of the twentieth century, additional components in sewage became sources of concern. Nitrates and phosphates could cause algal blooms that offload toxins, or, when rotted, consume dissolved oxygen, suffocating aquatic life. Organic molecules from various industrial and domestic sources also have had long-term negative impacts to both public health and environmental quality. Heavy metals, such as arsenic, cadmium, chromium, copper, iron, lead and mercury, even in minute concentrations, are toxic to people. Radioactive isotopes, such as radium and radon, have appeared as contaminants in South Jersey environments. Today, pesticides, fertilizers, manufactured chemicals and pharmaceuticals in sewage are presenting new problems. New treatment techniques have evolved to deal with these new challenges.

HAS SOUTH JERSEY CLEANED UP ITS ACT?

The number of cases of waterborne infectious diseases has dropped precipitously. The few cases that do occur are now treatable with antibiotics and pre-emptive

Date Built	Number of Plants	Screens	Sedimentation	Filtration	Surface Application	Disinfection	Date Built	Number of Plants	Screens	Sedimentation	Filtration	Surface Application	Disinfection
Bays/Back Bays							*Land Applications & Lakes*						
1904	1		1				1909	2	2	1	2		1
1909	2		2	1			1911	1	1				
1910	4		4			4	?	3	2		3		1
1911	3		2			3	*Subsurface Discharge*						
1912	2		2			2	1912	2			2		
1913	3		3			3	?	1			1		
Ocean							*Streams and Rivers*						
1903	1	1					*Flows into Delaware Bay*						
1905	2	2					1901	4	4	2		4	1
1906	1	1					1908			1			1
1907	2	2					1911			1			2
1909	5	5					*Delaware River*						
1910	2	2				1	1892	10	9	5		4	
1911	3	3					*Delaware R. Tributaries*						
1912	1	1					1897	19	17	13	2	1	
1913	1	1				1	*Flows into the Ocean*						
1914	1		1	1		1	1894	2	6	4	1	2	
?	2	2					*Flows into Raritan Bay*						
							1910	2	2	1		1	

Table 8. Wastewater-sewage disposal in South Jersey.[52]

inoculations. The turbidity and odor of the water supply is all but eliminated through aeration and the filtration of particulates and organic matter at its source. The removal of iron particles (i.e., rust and iron staining) has also, to some extent, been achieved. But certain essentially natural threats to water quality persist, including saltwater contamination and hydrogen sulfide gas odor near the shore.

Threats from human activities have expanded. The change from one water source to another, each with its own water chemistry, without treatment adjustments, has and may still cause the leaching of heavy metals from the pipes that carry water to individual homes and businesses, such as occurred in Flint, Michigan, c. 2015. Infiltration of surface contaminants into water supplies has persisted. Manure piles on farms, once recognized by the Health Department as a threat, are largely eliminated. Accidental spills of toxic chemicals still occur, but more modern threats have developed. Contaminant infiltration from legal and illegal landfills prompted the passage of the Clean Water Act and the *Superfund* program in the 1970s. Similarly, the contamination of water supplies from fertilizers, pesticides, chemical storage tanks and industrial wastes have been recognized with steps taken to eliminate them. More recently, the threat of pharmaceuticals to water quality has received recognition. These newer threats are proving more difficult and more expensive to eliminate.

While South Jersey has successfully eliminated the initial causes that threatened public health through its water supply, an expanding number of new threats, more difficult to eliminate, have been recognized. Past threats by infectious, waterborne diseases resulted in the development of new technologies and governmental structures to deal with these newer threats. This would have been impossible if all homeowners were still responsible for their own utilities.

Treatment Method	Atlantic	Burlington	Camden	Cape May	Cumberland	Gloucester	Monmouth	Ocean	Salem	Total
Sanitary Wastewater	2	30	2	5	3	5	19	2	8	76
Industrial Wastewater	1	10	2	3	8	18	9	2	9	62
Combined Sewer System	0	0	3	0	0	0	0	0	0	3
Dental Onsite Wastewater System	0	13	4	4	2	1	16	6	5	51
Land Application Biosolids	1	2	0	18	2	0	0	1	1	25
Land Application Industrial Residues	1	0	0	0	0	0	3	0	1	5
Land Application-Food Processing Res.	0	2	1	0	8	5	1	0	0	17
Clean Up-Petroleum Products	0	4	2	1	1	5	5	2	0	20
Clean Up-Remediation	0	1	1	1	0	2	3	0	0	8
Sanitary Subsurface Disposal	57	43	13	53	21	23	38	38	15	301
Discharge to Groundwater	8	33	9	19	18	26	36	15	10	174
Potable Water Basins & Drying Beds	0	5	0	1	0	0	10	0	2	18
Reed Bed-Residuals Treatment	0	2	1	0	0	0	3	0	0	6
Line Surface Impoundments	0	2	0	0	0	0	3	0	1	6
Animal Feeding Operations	0	1	0	0	0	2	1	0	1	5
Resource Transfer Facility	0	1	0	0	1	0	0	0	0	2
Non-Contact Cooling Water	0	0	0	0	1	1	0	1	1	4
Wastewater Beneficial Reuse	0	4	1	0	0	3	3	1	1	13
Wood Recycling	0	0	0	0	0	0	0	0	1	1
Concrete Products Manufacture	5	7	7	2	5	2	17	8	3	56

Table 9. Current treatment plants by county and method of treatment.[53]

ACKNOWLEDGMENTS

Several people were very helpful in the preparation of this manuscript. Members of the West Jersey History Roundtable provided probing questions and off color title suggestions during its preparation. Special thanks go to my wife, Liz Snowdon, for critiquing this manuscript and making important suggestions and corrections.

ABOUT THE AUTHOR

Claude Epstein is a founding faculty member of Stockton University and co-founder of the Environmental Studies Program and the Professional Master's Degree in Environmental Science. He received his Ph.D. from Brown University in Geology and taught at Stockton from 1971 to 2011. He was instrumental in studying the impact of Stockton's experimental sprayfields, the University's first sewage treatment system, in use from 1972 through 1982. He was also part of the team that examined the impact of Stockton's geothermal well field. As a hydrogeologist he worked on the aquifers, streams and wetlands of South Jersey. His book-length study of the environmental and cultural history of South Jersey rivers is being prepared for publication by the South Jersey Culture & History Center.

ENDNOTES

1 Edwin Chadwick, *Report on the Sanitary Conditions of the Laboring Population and the Means of Improvement* (London, 1842).

2 Peter O. Wacker, *Land & People: A Cultural Geography of Preindustrial New Jersey: Origins and Settlement Patterns* (New Brunswick: Rutgers University Press, 1975), 138.

3 U.S. Government Census for 2010, accessed June, 2017, http://www.census.gov/geo/www/tiger/index.html.

4 Steele Mabon Kennedy, John T. Cunningham, Captain Andrea Lippi, Bertrand P. Boucher, and Patricia S. Merlo, *The New Jersey Almanac and Travel Guide* (Cedar Grove, NJ: The New Jersey Almanac, Inc., 1968), 150–51; New Jersey Department of Labor, *New Jersey Population Trends 1790 to 2000* (Trenton: New Jersey State Data Center, 2001), 23.

5 David L. Cowen, *Medicine and Health in New Jersey: A History*, vol. 10, New Jersey Historical Series (Princeton: D. Van Nostrand Company, Inc., 1964), 24–39.

6 Cowen, *Medicine and Health in New Jersey*, 2.

7 Kenrad E. Nelson and Carolyn F. Williams, *Infectious Disease Epidemiology*, third edition (Burlington, MA: Jones & Bartlett Learning, 2014), 6–13.

8 American Society of Microbiology, *Significant Events in Microbiology 1861–1999* (2013), accessed June, 2017, https://www.asm.org/index.php/.../7852-significant-events-in-microbiology-since-1861.

9 Nelson and Williams, *Infectious Disease Epidemiology*, 9.

10 Charles E. Rosenberg, *The Cholera Years: The United States in 1832, 1849, and 1866* (Chicago: University of Chicago Press, 1962), 1.

11 John M. Woodworth, *Cholera Epidemic of 1873 in the United States* (Washington, Treasury Department, Supervising Surgeon's Office, 1875), 543–62.

12 Woodworth, *Cholera Epidemic of 1873*, 582.

13 Woodworth, *Cholera Epidemic of 1873*, 608–612.

14 G. F. Pyle, "The Diffusion of Cholera in the United States in the Nineteenth Century," *Geographical Analysis* 1, no. 1 (1969): 59–75.

15 Woodworth, *Cholera Epidemic of 1873*, 636–37.

16 Stuart Galishoff, "Cholera in Newark, New Jersey," *Journal of the History of Medicine*, XXV, 438–48.

17 Woodworth, *Cholera Epidemic of 1873*, 662.

18 Woodworth, *Cholera Epidemic of 1873*, 11, 445.

19 New Jersey Board of Health, *Twenty-Fourth Annual Report of the Board of Health for the State of New Jersey for the Year 1900* (Trenton: John L. Murphy, Publishing Co., 1901), 8.

20 New Jersey Board of Health, *Thirty-Six through Eighty-Fourth Annual Reports* (1913–1962).

21 New Jersey Board of Health, *Thirty-Fourth Annual Report of the Board of Health for the State of New Jersey for the Year 1910* (Trenton: State Gazette Publishing Co., 1911), 104–106.

22 New Jersey Board of Health, *Thirty-Six through Eighty-Fourth Annual Reports* (1913–1962).

23 New Jersey Department of Health, *Twenty-Fourth Annual Report of the Board of Health of the State of New Jersey and the Report of the Bureau of Vital Statistics for the Year 1900* (Trenton: John L. Murphy Publishers, 1901), 141–43.

24 David M. Oshinsky, *Polio: An American Story* (New York: Oxford University Press, 2005), 12; New Jersey Board of Health, *Thirty-Fourth Annual Report of the Board of Health for the State of New Jersey for the Year 1910* (Trenton: State Gazette Publishing Co., 1911), 104–106.

25 New Jersey Board of Health, *Thirty-Six through Eighty-Fourth Annual Reports* (1913–1962).

26 Peter H. Gleick, ed., *Water in Crisis: A Guide to the World's Fresh Water Resources* (New York: Oxford University Press, 1993), 373–78.

27 Cowen, *Medicine and Health in New Jersey*, 79–90.

28 New Jersey Board of Health, *Fourth Annual Report of the Board of Health for the State of New Jersey* (Camden, NJ: printed by Sinnickson Chew, 1881), 119–21.

29 Judith Walzer Leavitt, *Typhoid Mary: Captive of the Public's Health* (Boston: Beacon Press, 1996).

30 New Jersey Board of Health, *Ninth, Annual Report of the Board of Health for the State of New Jersey for the Year 1885* (Trenton: printed by John L. Murphy, 1886), 217; New Jersey Board of Health, *Twelfth Annual Report of the Board of Health for the State of New Jersey for the Year 1888* (Trenton: printed by John L. Murphy, 1889), 119–21.

31 New Jersey Board of Health, *Eighteenth Annual Report of the Board of Health for the State of New Jersey for the Year 1894* (Trenton: MacCrellish & Quigley, 1895), 35, 41.

32 New Jersey Board of Health, *Nineteenth Annual Report of the Board of Health for the State of New Jersey for the Year 1895* (Trenton: printed by John L. Murphy, 1896), 6–7.

33 New Jersey Board of Health, *Twentieth Annual Report of the Board of Health for the State of New Jersey for the Year 1896* (Trenton: printed by John L. Murphy, 1897), 22–25.

34 New Jersey Board of Health, *Twenty-Ninth Annual Report of the Board of Health for the State of New Jersey for the Year 1905* (Trenton: printed by John L. Murphy, 1906), 162.

35 New Jersey Board of Health, *Twenty-Ninth Annual Report of the Board of Health for the State of New Jersey for the Year 1905*, 160–64.

36 New Jersey Board of Health, *Thirty-Fourth Annual Report of the Board of Health for the State of New Jersey for the Year 1910* (Trenton: State Gazette Publishing Co., 1911), 103.

37 New Jersey Board of Health, *Twenty-Fourth Annual Report of the Board of Health for the State of New Jersey for the Year 1900* (Trenton: printed by John L. Murphy, 1901), 94–107.

38 New Jersey Board of Health, *Thirty-Fourth Annual Report of the Board of Health for the State of New Jersey for the Year 1910*, 217.

39 New Jersey Board of Health, *Thirty-Fifth Annual Report of the Board of Health for the State of New Jersey for the Year 1911*, (Trenton: State Gazette Publishing Co., 1911), 125.

40 New Jersey Board of Health, *Thirty-Fourth Annual Report of the Board of Health for the State of New Jersey for the Year 1910*, 128–32.

41 New Jersey Board of Health, *Twenty-Fourth Annual Report of the Board of Health for the State of New Jersey for the Year 1900* (Trenton: John L. Murphy, Publishing Co., 1901), 253–87.

42 C. M. Epstein, "Discovery of the Aquifers of the New Jersey Coastal Plain in the Nineteenth Century," *History of Geophysics*, eds. E. R. Landa and S. Ince, vol. III (1987): 69–73.

43 New Jersey Board of Health, *Twenty-Fourth Annual Report for the State of New Jersey for 1900* (Trenton: J. L. Murphy Publishing Co., 1901), 110–254. John C. Flood, *General History of Plumbing Timeline*, accessed February 2017, https://www.johncflood.com/blog/general/history-of-plumbing-timeline.

44 New Jersey Board of Health, *Twenty-Sixth Annual Report for the State of New Jersey for 1902* (Trenton: J. L. Murphy Publishing Co., 1903), 345–50.

45 New Jersey Board of Health, *Forty-First Annual Report for the State of New Jersey for 1918*, (Trenton: State of New Jersey, 1920), 106–107.

46 New Jersey Board of Health, *Forty-First Annual Report for the State of New Jersey for 1918* (Trenton: State of New Jersey, 1920), 108.

47 New Jersey Board of Health, *Forty-First Annual Report for the State of New Jersey for 1918*, 103–105.

48 New Jersey Board of Health, *Forty-First Annual Report for*

the State of New Jersey for 1918, 109–112.

49 U.S. Environmental Protection Agency, *Primer for Municipal Wastewater Treatment Systems* (Washington: Office of Wastewater Management, 2004), EPA 832-R-04-001

50 New Jersey Board of Health, *Thirty-Seventh Annual Report for the State of New Jersey for 1913* (Paterson, NJ: News Printing Co., 1914), 509.

51 New Jersey Board of Health, *Thirty-Fourth Annual Report*

for the State of New Jersey for 1910, 361.

52 Division of Water Quality, *NJPDES Data Base Management*, accessed March 2017, http://www.nj.gov/dep/dwq/database.htm.

53 New Jersey Department of Environmental Protection, accessed June 2017, http://www.nj.gov/dep/commissioner/vision-priorities.pdf.

Burlington, New Jersey, Water Works. (Upper left) In the late nineteenth century, the City of Burlington responded to the need for a modern water delivery system for its residents and businesses. While the city had a private company as early as 1805 distributing low-pressure water on a limited basis, Burlington officials took their responsibilities seriously and constructed the first phase of a new brick pumping station with filtration beds in 1881. Additions to the building continued until 1897, when the final section, shown here, completed the complex.

(Upper right) To power the new pumping station, city officials contracted for boilers and high duty pumping engines from the Holly-Gaskill Company of Lockport, New York, at a cost of $5,000. Invented by Harvey F. Gaskill in 1881, this type of engine—a rotative beam non-receiver compound engine—became a fixture in many waterworks across the country. In this view, Burlington's proud engineer stands in front of his spotless engines.

(Left) By 1891, the city's Water Works Commission had ordered a plate-iron standpipe from Morris, Tasker & Company of Philadelphia and had it erected at the waterworks to increase system pressure. The 129-foot-high vertical reservoir had a maximum capacity of 286,000 gallons of water. The City of Burlington continued to source its distributive water from the Delaware River until 1954, when artesian wells, located on Burlington Island, came on line and the river intakes were closed. The city abandoned their old waterworks during the late 1970s, when a new facility just upriver became operational. The old waterworks underwent demolition within the past three years.

Stockton University Welcomes Heather Perez:
Special Collections Librarian and Archivist

Amy Krieger

It is an article of faith that every student who has attended college or university has, at one time or other, sought out the library to study, complete research, or, at least, to use the printers. Libraries, and the librarians who staff them, are essential to academic success. Whenever students need help with a research question, cannot find a book, or need assistance with those jammed printers, they turn to librarians.

College students may not appreciate the variety of duties completed by librarians within a university setting. The Richard E. Bjork Library of Stockton University holds tens of thousands of books and journals, along with helpful reference material, available in a mix of print and electronic forms, all catalogued, organized, and made available by hard-working librarians.

Heather Perez, the newest librarian to join Stockton, was hired during the summer of 2017 as the University's first full-time Special Collections Librarian and Archivist.

Perez completed her undergraduate degree at the College of William and Mary in Virginia where she graduated with a Bachelor's degree in Government and a minor in History. At the close of her undergraduate career, she realized that her love of research outweighed her love

Heather Perez.

of government and history. She found the perfect field in Special Collections and enrolled at the University of Maryland where she completed her Masters of Library Science degree.

While in graduate school, she worked at the National Archives before moving on to the Atlantic City Free Public Library after graduation. During her time in Atlantic City, Perez gained positive community notice organizing an award-winning Atlantic City Experience exhibition as well as serving as historical consultant for the HBO show *Boardwalk Empire.*

As Special Collections Librarian, Perez curates Stockton's growing South Jersey collections, including print and manuscript documents, rare books, maps, photographs, and sound recordings—all related to the eight southernmost counties of New Jersey.

She is also the University archivist in charge of preserving and making available documents and materials related to the history of Stockton. Louise Tillstrom and other library staff ably assist Perez, as do student interns and student workers.

In addition to these duties, Perez also investigates possible acquisitions, answers questions from patrons, and posts to social media announcements of events or

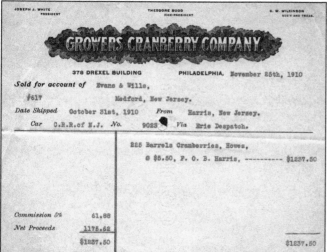

(Top left) Postcard image of the Estell Glassworks, c. 1906, in the Rebecca Estell Bourgeois collection. (Bottom left) 1910 invoice for cranberries sold for Evans & Wills, in the Evans and Wills collection. (Top Right) Compact disks in the Cape May Jazz Festival collection.

interesting material that can be found within the collections. Major donations to the growing South Jersey collections are described below.

Perez believes that libraries are central to the collaborative and digital nature of modern education. She also believes that, as a twenty-first century librarian, it is her responsibility to help make information accessible to all comers, whether in person or online. Special Collections is, therefore, working to digitize historic materials that will be easily accessed online. Throughout

THE COLLECTIONS

The William W. Leap collection preserving the history and culture of South Jersey. Approximately 1,265 titles in a variety of formats: monographs, annuals, maps, atlases, newspaper and magazine articles.

The David C. Munn collection of South Jersey literature and history. An extensive collection of novels, poetry, historical texts and ephemera related to New Jersey, with a clear focus on the published works of South Jersey.

The R. Marilyn Schmidt/Buzby collection. Documents pertaining to the historic Chatsworth General Store and surrounding Pine Barrens: letters, invoices, teacher vouchers, postcards, photos, newspaper clippings, photographs of the restoration of the store in 1998–1999.

Pine Barrens/Pinelands collections covering the history, geography, agriculture and ecology of the region, including documents and meeting minutes issued by the Pinelands Commission. Recently augmented by the Pinelands Collection formerly held by Burlington County College.

The Budd Wilson collection. A range of materials pertaining to Martha Furnace, Batsto, and the Mullica

River valley, with special focus on the letters of the poet Emma Van Sant Moore to A. Hollis Koster and documentation related to Koster, who was both a poet and botanist.

The Chew account books. A collection of account books, dating from 1830–1874, kept by Israel Chew, a store and tavern keeper, and William Chew, a blacksmith. The accounts contain references to numerous families across Camden and Burlington Counties and to Batsto and Atsion.

The Rebecca Estell Bourgeois collection. Several hundred documents related to the Estell-Bourgeois family in southeastern Atlantic County, New Jersey, dating from 1723–1930, including letters documenting the Estell glassworks in the mid-nineteenth century; nautical documents pertaining to shipping, shipbuilding and ship outfitting along Stephen's Creek, in the Tuckahoe River; and hundreds of land deeds.

Evans & Wills collection. Business records of the Evans & Wills Company, Inc., a family-owned berry farm (mainly cranberries, some blueberries) that continued nearly 100 years from 1868 to the mid 1960s. The majority of the collection consists of detailed records from 1930,

Welcome Heather Perez

Stockton's library, one sees the melding of paper and digital technology. Visitors to the Bjork Library will find up-to-date computers and online databases, but they will also find shelves of circulating books, reference materials, and the materials of Special Collections, which do not circulate.

Heather Perez is a teaching librarian who eagerly works with the interns she supervises. She is, of course, happy to help any students or community members who find their way to Stockton's Special Collections and Archives, which are open Monday through Friday from 8 am to 4 pm. Perez suggests making an appointment via telephone (609-652-4555) or email (Heather.Perez@stockton.edu) so that she can research and retrieve applicable material before you arrive at the library to maximize your available research time.

(Right) A page from Elizabeth B. Alton's scrapbook, in the Elizabeth B. Alton papers. (Following page, top) Items from the John Henry "Pop" Lloyd Committee collection. (Middle) A view of the Reading Room. (Bottom) Photograph of soundboard, in the Stockton University Archives. (Background image) Miscellaneous manuscript materials from the Rebecca Estell Bourgeois collection.

---

the date of incorporation, through the dissolution of the company.

The Steve Eichinger collection. Extensive material related to the Wading River area during the nineteenth and early twentieth centuries, including several field books of Samuel Downs, surveyor and conveyancer, describing his work in the field as he surveyed in Atlantic and Burlington Counties; hand-drawn survey maps; deeds; and the McKeen Day Books, recording riverine shipments up and down the Wading River from the mid to late nineteenth century.

The John Henry "Pop" Lloyd Committee collection. The committee's archives, artwork, and supporting materials dedicated to preserving the history of Negro League Baseball.

Cape May Jazz Festival collection which covers the event's history from 1994–2010. The collection includes artwork, promotional materials, and several hundred music CDs.

The Bernard Sless collection on the history of the region and development of the gaming industry in Atlantic City.

Elizabeth B. Alton papers. Materials related to the life and work of Mrs. Alton, member of the first Board of Trustees of Stockton University and an important figure in the drive to build the college in South Jersey that became Stockton.

William J. Hughes papers. Materials related to the career of William J. "Bill" Hughes, who served as a member of the U.S. House of Representatives, representing New Jersey's Second Congressional District, including scrapbooks, clippings, speeches & statements, press releases, and photographs.

The Seaview Country Club collection. The collection comprises items gathered by the Seaview between 1914 and 2003, including photographs, postcards, menus, realia, and more.

Historic map collection: a range of intriguing maps that show the development of South Jersey over time.

ABOUT THE AUTHOR. Amy Krieger is a Stockton University Literature major who plans to pursue a masters degree in library and information science. She is currently working in Special Collections on the Cape May Jazz Festival collection.

THIS INDENTURE made this 16th day of August in
of our Lord one thousand eight hundred and thirteen 1813 BETWEEN Jonathan Scull of the Township
in the County of Cumberland and State of New Jersey and Elizabeth his wife
of the City of Philadelphia

said party of the first part, for and in consideration of the sum of
money of the United States of America to him in hand,

The Executors of the Estate of

1842		
April 24	Costs of Suit against Milner	3/6
Mar 29	1 Shade Bill for Painting	13.00
January	Water Rent	5.10
July 14	Taxes	19.00
Aught 14	W Cansler - Paperhanging	12.00
" 30	Goodwill Bill for Painting	30.00
Sept 1	Brick Layers Bill	1.00
	House	3.50
	Carpenter Bill	1.18	77

NATIONAL BASEBALL HALL OF FAME AND MUSEUM

Shades of Glory

LAWRENCE D. HOGAN
WITH A FOREWORD BY JULES TYGIEL

THE NEGRO LEAGUES AND THE STORY
of AFRICAN-AMERICAN BASEBALL

"On behalf of my family and the other families of Negro league
players, I wish to thank the authors for creating this outstanding
tribute. Words fail to express how truly honored we feel to know
that these ball players' accomplishments are being recognized in
such an exceptional manner. These were amazing athletes who
in their final days simply wanted to be remembered."
—Linda Paige Shelby, daughter of Satchel Paige

THE POP LLOYD
COLLECTION

City Jan 20th 1
W. E. Cole
Dear
I have got answer
my uncle in New J
he say his Grand Fa
name was William
two Brothers whose na
was John and Johnat
Johnathan was what
called a Tory and he

Ghost Forests in the Mullica Valley:
Indicators of Sea-Level Rise

Kenneth W. Able, Jennifer Walker and Benjamin P. Horton

The Mullica Valley is a relatively undisturbed ecosystem that has recovered from a 150–200 year period of resource-based industrialization that began in the late 1600s. It is currently protected from further environmental damage through federal and state forests, wildlife management areas, and parks, as well as the low human population density in the watershed.[1] As a result, the Mullica Valley is the cleanest watershed in New Jersey and one of the most pristine on the Atlantic Coast of the U.S. For all of these reasons, it provides a unique baseline from which to judge the effects of sea-level rise.

The Mullica Valley is a good indicator of sea-level rise, because it is home to extensive Atlantic white cedar forests scattered throughout the Valley that are at risk from both direct saltwater and indirect freshwater inundation due to rising sea levels (Fig. 1). These cedar forests still resemble those described in the nineteenth century by Alexander Wilson, an early American ornithologist.

> These swamps . . . appear as if they occupied the former channel of some choked up river, stream, lake, or arm of the sea. The appearance they present to the stranger is singular. A front of tall and per-fectly straight trunks, rising to the height of fifty or sixty feet without a limb, and crowded in every direction, their tops so closely woven together as to shut out the day, spreading the gloom of perpetual twilight below. On a nearer approach, they are found to rise out of the water, which, from the impregnation of the fallen leaves and roots of the cedars, is of the color of brandy. Amidst this bottom of congregated springs, the ruins of the former forest lie piled in every state of confusion.[2]

Atlantic white cedar is intolerant of salt water and, therefore, a good indicator of long and short term exposure to salt water in estuarine waters.[3] Laboratory experiments indicate very low salt levels can reduce and kill seedlings.[4] Observations by those who raise the seedlings for planting have observed mortality if exposed to two or three flood tide cycles of salt water.[5] Sea-level rise can also indirectly cause the death of Atlantic

Mullica Valley Wetlands
Marsh Dominated by Salt Water Cordgrass
Marsh Dominated by Salt Hay Grass
Atlantic White Cedar Wetlands
Common Reed Phragmites Dominate Wetland

0   3   6   12 Miles

Fig. 1. Current distribution of living Atlantic white cedar in the Mullica Valley. Note the frequency with which it occurs along freshwater streams in the upper portion of the watershed.

white cedar by increasing groundwater tables, allowing freshwater to inundate and drown the forests from within.[6]

Atlantic white cedar can reach large sizes and grow for over 1000 years (Fig. 2), based on early research by George H. Cook of Rutgers University.[7] Even after dying, Atlantic white cedar refuses to decay, especially when buried in the oxygen free sediments as has often occurred in the Mullica Valley and elsewhere in New Jersey, such as in the Meadowlands in northeastern New Jersey.[8] As an indication of resilience, cedar has commonly been "mined" from bog sediments, sometimes many feet deep, and has been taken directly to sawmills to be cut up for a variety of products.[9] In fact, when massive buried cedar logs were discovered up to 40 feet deep in the marsh sediments, while the Garden State Parkway bridge over the Mullica River was under construction in the early 1950s, these logs were sold to a mill and turned into valuable cedar shingles.[10] Further, this fascinating

tree has had high monetary value since the colonization of the area by Europeans, beginning over 300 years ago. Its monetary value stems from its use as ship masts, building lumber, shingles and furniture.

MODERN GHOST FORESTS

Ghost forests are standing dead trees that have been killed by exposure to salt water. Their frequency has been increasing in recent decades. They can be seen along roadsides, in creeks, or from the air as observed from a helicopter during fall 2016 at Otter Pond in Big Creek near Port Republic (Fig. 3). Standing dead trees are obvious at the edge of the marsh; it is clear that the salt marsh is invading the forest at the same time that the trees are dying. These dead trees can be pines or oaks, typical of the Pine Barrens, but the most prominent are often Atlantic white cedars, because they remain upright for long periods of time. These standing dead cedars are occurring with increasing frequency as sea levels are rising and the salt waters are invading further up the Mullica Valley. The evidence for salt water induced mortality is based on long term observations, stretching from the late 1800s.[11]

Corroboration is easily observable in the Mullica, Wading, and Bass rivers as well as many of the smaller tributaries in the Mullica Valley. A helicopter flight over the Valley in 2017 documented this clearly (Fig. 4). These helicopter observations show the lateral extent of the dead trees further from the water's edge, while closer inspection from kayaks in remote creeks, which are tributaries to the Mullica River, reveals that these ghost forests are frequent and consist of dead standing trees surrounded by the invading marsh (Fig 4). The ghost forests are not evident lower in the estuary, where presumably the environment has remained too salty for cedar forests in the recent past and where ghost forests may be preserved deeper under the sediment.

Fig. 2. Atlantic white cedar that formerly grew in the Great Swamp of Green Bank State Forest (now Wharton State Forest), New Gretna, New Jersey, and fell in the hurricane of November 1950. The photo was taken by A. Hollis Koster prior to 1920. The man is the late John Simpkins of Green Bank, holding a six-foot, two-man saw. *Courtesy of Charles Bell, Lower Bank, New Jersey.*

An easily accessible example of a ghost forest occurs in Nacote Creek at Port Republic, where this tributary off the Mullica River is dammed (Fig. 5). Just above the dam and lake are thriving Atlantic white cedar forests. Below the dam, from the road that passes south of the creek, one can observe ghost forests

Fig. 3. Current landscape of Otter Pond in Big Creek, a tributary of the Mullica River near Port Republic, with standing dead Atlantic white cedar at the marsh—upland edge.

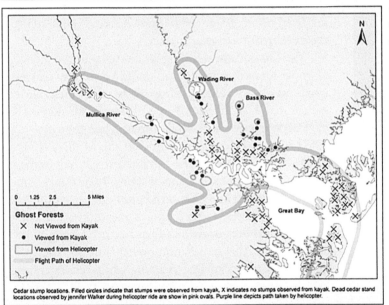

Fig. 4. Distribution of recent, standing dead ghost forests in the Mullica Valley, as indicated by red circles and ovals, based on a helicopter flight on May 19, 2017 (area enclosed in purple). Filled circles indicate that stumps were observed from kayak. X indicates no stumps observed from kayak or motorboat.

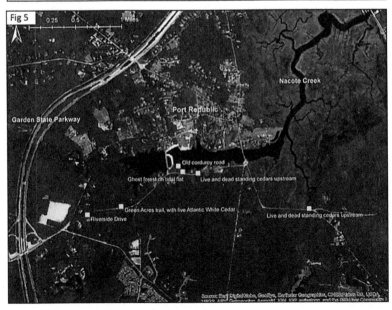

Fig 5. Google Earth image of Nacote Creek, a tributary of the Mullica River, at Port Republic, an easily accessible area that indicates several stages in local sea-level rise and status of Atlantic white cedar in areas indicated with filled squares.

being formed where smaller creeks reach up into the forest (Fig. 6). Within a few yards one can see living forest in the background, dead standing cedars in front

Fig. 6. Photograph of transition from living Atlantic white cedars in background to standing dead Atlantic white cedars in front of them, and *Phragmites* marsh invading the forest along a small stream, a tributary of Nacote Creek, at Riverside Road in Port Republic. See Fig. 5 for other details.

of that, and marsh grass (*Phragmites*) invading the former forest. The most recent example of ghost forest formation is from Superstorm Sandy when this storm pushed salt water up the estuary, above the typical freshwater-saltwater interface, and flooded a portion of marsh that was surrounded by a road with higher elevation.[12] This resulted, months later, with many dead Atlantic white cedars on one side of the road and living cedars on the other side (Fig. 7).

The timeline of flooding events is critical to interpretation of the formation of ghost forests and a means to evaluate their relationship with rates of sea-level rise. Global mean sea-level has risen ~7 inches at an average rate of ~0.05 inches per year from 1901–1990.[13] Based on tide gauge data, local relative sea levels in New Jersey recorded a ~16 inch rise during the twentieth century, rising at a rate of 0.12 inches per year since ~1850.[14] The instrumental record of relative sea level

in New Jersey begins in 1911, with the installation of the Atlantic City tide gauge and is currently recording rises in excess of 0.16 inches/year. Rates of sea-level rise in New Jersey are greater than the global mean due to both ground water withdrawal and New Jersey's location in regards to an extinct ice sheet known as the Laurentide Ice Sheet. During the last glaciation (~20,000 years ago), land beneath the Laurentide Ice Sheet in northern Canada subsided and land at the periphery of the ice sheet, such as the U.S. mid-Atlantic coastline, uplifted in a feature known as the peripheral forebulge. After the melting of the Laurentide Ice Sheet, a reverse of this land motion seesaw occurred, causing a collapse of the forebulge and land subsidence along the U.S. mid-Atlantic coastline. The collapse of the peripheral forebulge and resulting subsidence caused relative sea-level rise in New Jersey to be greater than the global average.[15] Therefore, the higher rates of sea-level rise experienced in New Jersey present an even greater threat to coastal forests.

We can get some feeling, at least, for the sequence of ghost forest formation and their invasion by marshes when we observe old corduroy roads, at low tide, buried within marsh sediments (Fig. 8). These roads may have been created in colonial times, when they provided access to the main channel of the Mullica River or when the areas were used to harvest salt hay in the "meadows" with horse drawn wagons.[16] Certainly some of these, evident in 1930s aerial photographs, imply that approximately one and a half feet of sediment deposited above the timbers in the road has occurred since those photographs. This sedimentation explains one mechanism for burial of ancient Atlantic white cedars and the formation of ancient "cedar cemeteries."

Fig. 7. Standing dead Atlantic white cedar forest (grey area) along the right side of the road to Lower Bank bridge resulting from Superstorm Sandy along the Mullica River.

ANCIENT GHOST FORESTS

"Cedar cemeteries" are found in several locations in the Mullica Valley. The ancient Atlantic white cedar died from exposure to salt water due to gradual sea-level rise over the past several thousand years. Sea level has been slowly rising in New Jersey mainly due to land subsidence with the melting of the Laurentide Ice Sheet.[17] Horton et al. accounted for additional local factors including sediment compaction and tidal range change and found that relative sea level rose at an average rate of 0.16 inches per year from 10,000–6000 years ago, 0.08 inches per year from 6000–2000 years ago, and 0.05 inches per year from 2000 years ago.[18] The twentieth-century rate of rise (0.12 inches per year) is the fastest rate of sea-level rise experienced for several thousand years.[19]

"Cedar cemeteries" have been preserved within the sediment, because of the resilient nature of the wood. But the accelerated sea-level rise of the twentieth and twenty-first centuries has enhanced erosion of the marsh edge and creeks, revealing previously buried ancient ghost forests. Our series of visual ground-truthing observations while paddling kayaks at low tides throughout the watershed over the last two years demonstrates this quite clearly (Fig. 4). The ancient ghost forests are most evident at or near the upper limits of the Mullica, Wading, and Bass rivers and Nacote Creek. The absence of ancient ghost forests in Great Bay and the lower Wading and Bass rivers is likely due to their burial under accumulated sediments over hundreds to thousands of years. Indeed, the massive trunks and timbers of ancient cedar trees were excavated from beneath 40 feet of sediment during the construction of the Garden State Parkway over the Mullica River.[20]

"Cedar cemeteries" have been found in the Bass River (Fig. 9) and in Otter Pond in Big Creek near Port

Fig. 9. Exposed ancient ghost forest of Atlantic white cedar stumps and logs due to sea level rise at low tide in the Bass River. Note the *Phragmites* marsh between the ghost forest and the upland forest.

Fig. 10. Exposed ancient ghost forest of Atlantic white cedar stumps and logs at low tide in the Otter Pond at Big Creek near Port Republic.

Fig. 8. Portion of an old corduroy road under marsh sediments in Jerry's Creek, a tributary of the Mullica River at end of Mannheim Road.

Fig. 11. Large stump of Atlantic white cedar exposed at low tide in the Otter Pond at Big Creek near Port Republic. The white portion of the kayak paddle is 18 inches long.

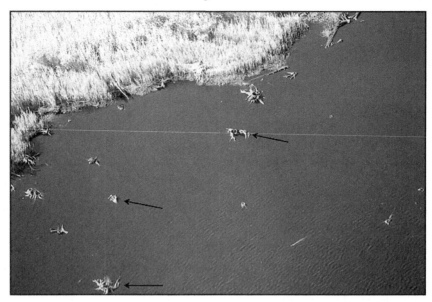

Fig. 12. Aerial image from a helicopter of Atlantic white cedar stumps in shallow waters of the Wading River.

Fig. 13. (Top) A small scale, current Google Earth image of Nacote Creek, a tributary of the Mullica River, below the dam. (Bottom) an aerial image of marsh development in the 1930s, which covers the ghost forest shown in Fig. 14. The red lines in both top and bottom images indicate the shoreline from 2017.

Fig. 14. Aerial image from a helicopter of the same area shown in Fig. 13. Note the former marsh between the open creek waters and Riverside Road on the left side of the image.

Fig. 15. Photograph of exposed ghost forest timbers at same location as in Fig. 14. *Courtesy of George Mattei.*

Republic (Fig. 10). Some of these cedars are of quite large size (Fig. 11). The same kind of recent exposure is evident in the Wading River where Atlantic white cedar stumps are visible from a helicopter at an eroding marsh edge (Fig. 12). At the same time, the acceleration in sea-level rise is allowing the marsh to expand elsewhere. This sea-level rise effect is especially obvious as it invades living Atlantic white cedars and kills the trees in the process. This marsh expansion is likely except where human construction prevents it from moving inland.

An early aerial photograph of the area at Nacote Creek at Port Republic puts recent ghost forest formation into a longer-term perspective (Fig. 13). In the 1930s, the shorelines on both sides of the creek below the dam were covered with extensive marshes. A 2016 aerial image (Fig. 14) shows that the creek is much wider. The north shoreline, closest to downtown Port Republic, was dredged and used as fill to create the higher ground where basketball and tennis courts sit today. On the south shore, the marsh has receded and almost reaches the nearby Riverside Road (Fig. 13, 14). On closer examination, it is clear that the receded area consists of exposed Atlantic white cedar

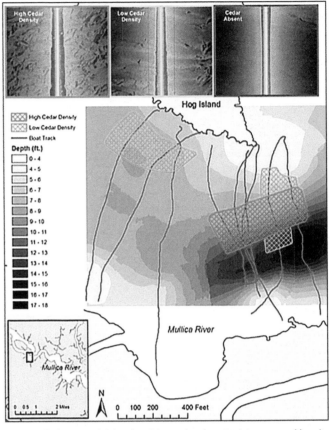

Fig. 17. Submerged Atlantic white cedar density (stumps and logs) determined by side-scan sonar observations south of Hog Islands in the Mullica River (see inset). Transects made by boat are shown as red lines. Side-scan sonar recorded 45 to 90 feet on both sides of the boat's course. Bathymetry derived from side-scan depth data.

timbers and stumps with remnants of the salt marsh identified in the 1930s (Fig. 15).

The timeline of ancient ghost forests in the Mullica Valley may extend quite far back in time. Besides those observed at low tide in many tributaries, there are others that are even deeper in salt waters of the river channels and thus likely even older. Submerged "cedar cemeteries" can be seen with side-scan sonar at three locations in the narrow channel (4–6 feet at high tide) of the Bass River (Fig. 16), in the channel (7–10 ft) of the Mullica River near Hog Islands (Fig. 17), and in the Wading River (Fig. 18). Where the submerged cedars occur in discrete clumps of differing densities, the logs range from 8.2–29.5 feet in length and 0.3–1.3 feet in height. Radiocarbon dating of dead cedar in a tidal flat area of Port Republic suggests that these trees date back to the mid-sixteenth to seventeenth centuries. In the upper Bass River, radiocarbon dates suggest ages of dead cedars from the early eighteenth century; further downstream in the Mullica, cedar dating suggests ages from the fifth century. The ages of these dead cedars demonstrate the process of how sea-level rise over time has pushed saltwater inland and created ghost forests.

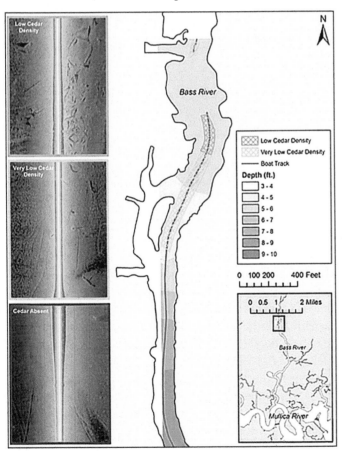

Fig. 16. Submerged Atlantic white cedar density (stumps and logs) determined by side-scan sonar observations in the Bass River (see inset). Transects made by boat are shown as red lines. Side-scan sonar recorded 45 to 90 feet on both sides of the boat's course. Bathymetry derived from side-scan depth data.

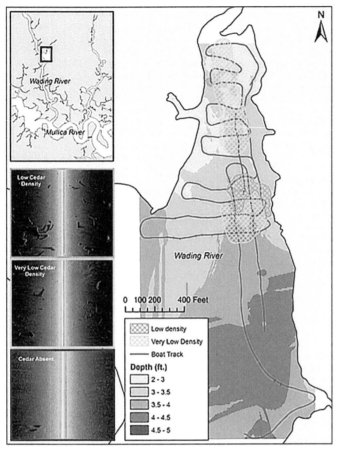

Fig. 18. Submerged Atlantic white cedar density (stumps and logs) determined by side-scan sonar observations in the Wading River (see inset). Transects made by boat are shown as red lines. Side-scan sonar recorded 45 to 90 feet on both sides of the boat's course. Bathymetry derived from side-scan depth data.

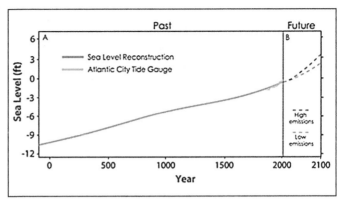

Fig. 19. Past and future sea-level change in New Jersey. (A) Sea-level reconstruction from Kemp et al. (2013) and instrumental record from Atlantic City tide gauge; (B) Twenty-first-century New Jersey regional projections of sea-level rise with "business-as-usual" greenhouse gas emissions (high emissions) and extremely strong cuts in emissions (low emissions) from Kopp et al. (2014).

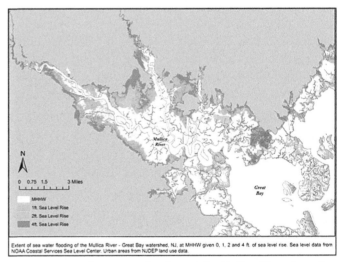

Fig. 20. Extent of seawater flooding of the Mullica River-Great Bay watershed, NJ, at Mean High High Water given 0, 1, 2, and 4 feet of sea level rise. Sea level data from NOAA Coastal Services Sea Level Center.

What is most remarkable, and obvious, about all of these examples is that these sites had to be in freshwater for the cedars to grow and survive, yet now they are exposed to salt waters continually or on every high tide.

More Ghost Forests in the Future

Sea-level will continue to rise globally as human-driven climate change increases global temperatures causing the ocean to expand and glaciers and ice sheets to melt. Projections for future sea-level rise by 2100 range from 20–51 inches with "business-as-usual" greenhouse gas emissions and 9–25 inches with extremely strong cuts in emissions (Fig. 19).[21] By the end of the twenty-first century the rate of rise could be as high as 0.3–0.7 inches per year (see Table 1 below). These high rates of sea-level rise will expand the area in the Mullica Valley that is exposed to higher salinities and

consistent and frequent immersion by estuarine waters (Fig. 20). Thus, we suggest, as sea-level rise continues to accelerate, more living Atlantic white cedar and other trees will be turned into standing dead ghost forests and this same sea-level rise will remove sediments from marsh edges and creeks and, in the process, expose more ancient Atlantic white cedars that are now buried in the marsh, as depicted in an early illustration for the edge of Delaware Bay (Fig. 21). A test of this suggestion will be possible in the Mullica Valley because the cedars above dams will not be exposed to these increasing salinities and flooding, such as above the dams in Port Republic and at Batsto Village.

Time	0–2000	1850–2000	1911–2016	2010–2030	2030–2050	2050–2100
Rate (inches per year)	0.05	0.12	0.16	0.2 to 0.4	0.3 to 0.5	0.3 to 0.7

Table 1. Rates of sea level rise for New Jersey.

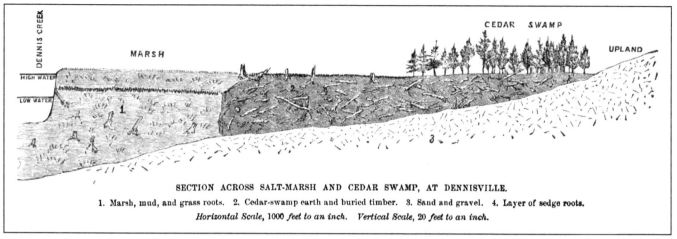

SECTION ACROSS SALT-MARSH AND CEDAR SWAMP, AT DENNISVILLE.

1. Marsh, mud, and grass roots.   2. Cedar-swamp earth and buried timber.   3. Sand and gravel.   4. Layer of sedge roots.

Horizontal Scale, 1000 *feet to an inch.*   *Vertical Scale*, 20 *feet to an inch.*

Fig. 21. Diagram indicating the burial of Atlantic white cedar forests over time: 1 = marsh, mud, and grass roots; 2 = cedar-swamp earth and buried timber; 3 = sand and gravel. Greatest vertical scale=20 feet. *George H. Cook,* Geology of the County of Cape May, State of New Jersey *(Trenton, NJ: The True American, 1857), 35.*

ACKNOWLEDGEMENTS

Numerous individuals willingly lent their expertise to this effort. Pat Filardi assisted greatly with the on-the-water observations from kayaks. Judy Redlawsk devoted her skills and her helicopter to observations from the air. Others provided expertise with Atlantic white cedar, George Zimmerman; archaeology, Budd Wilson; photographs, George Mattei; and local knowledge of the historical landscape, Gary Giberson and the Tuckerton Historical Society. Staff at the Rutgers University Marine Field Station (RUMFS), especially Ryan Larum and Maggie Shaw, assisted in the gathering of literature and preparation of maps and images. Funding for Jennifer Walker's Ph.D. comes from the National Science Foundation (OCE 1458904), the Community Foundation of New Jersey, and David and Arleen McGlade. This is Earth Observatory of Singapore Contribution 170.

ABOUT THE AUTHORS

Ken Able is a Distinguished Professor in the Department of Marine and Coastal Sciences and Director of the Marine Field Station at Rutgers University. His interests are diverse and include the life history and ecology of fishes with emphasis on habitat quality as well as the natural history of the Mullica Valley.

Jennifer Walker is a Ph.D. candidate in Oceanography in the Department of Marine and Coastal Sciences at Rutgers University. Her research focuses on the spatial and temporal variability of relative sea level in New Jersey during the past several thousand years.

Benjamin P. Horton is a Professor in the Department of Marine and Coastal Sciences, Rutgers University, and Associate Chair of the Asian School of the Environment, Nanyang Technological University, Singapore. He studies sea level of the past to provide a context for the future.

ENDNOTES

1   Kenneth W. Able and Gabriel Coia, "The Recovery of New Jersey's Mullica Valley," *Underwater Naturalist* 32, no. 2 (2017): 36–43.

2   Alexander Wilson, Charles Lucian Bonaparte, and William Jardine, *American Ornithology; or, The Natural History of the Birds of the United States*, in 3 vol., vol. 3 (London: Whittaker, Treacher & Arnott, 1832), 51.

3   Earl R. Rosenwinkel, "Vegetational History of a New Jersey Tidal Marsh, Bog, and Vicinity," *The Bulletin* 9, no. 1 (1964): 1–20; Ekaterina Sedia and George L. Zimmerman, "Effects of Salinity and Flooding on Atlantic White-Cedar Seedlings," paper presented at *The Ecology and Management of Atlantic White-Cedar Symposium 2006* (Atlantic City, NJ) June 6–8, 2006; John E. Pearce, *Heart of the Pines*, revised edition (Hammonton, NJ: Batsto Citizens Committee, Inc., 2000), 872.

4   Sedia and Zimmerman, "Effects of Salinity and Flooding on Atlantic White-Cedar Seedlings."

5   Terry O'Leary, personal communication.

6   Glen Carleton, USGS, personal communication.

7   George H. Cook, *Geology of New Jersey* (Newark, NJ: Board of Managers, 1868).

8   George L. Zimmermann and Kristin A. Mylecraine, "Reconstruction of an Old Growth Atlantic White Cedar Stand in the Hackensack Meadowlands of New Jersey: Preliminary Results," *Atlantic White Cedar Restoration Ecology and Management, Proceedings of a Symposium Christopher Newport University, Newport News, VA May 31–June 2, 2000*, eds. Robert B. Atkinson, Robert T. Belcher, David A. Brown, and James E. Perry (2003): 125–35.

9   Harry Bischoff Weiss and Grace M. Weiss, *Some Early Industries of New Jersey (Cedar Mining, Tar, Pitch, Turpentine, Salt Hay)* (Trenton, NJ: New Jersey Agricultural Society, 1965), 70.

10   S. Leifreid, personal communication.

11   Cook, *Geology of New Jersey*; Pearce, *Heart of the Pines*.

12   George Zimmerman, Judith Turk, and Claude Epstein, "Hurricane Sandy Salt Water Damage to Atlantic White-Cedar Hypothesis" (In preparation).

13   Carling C. Hay, Eric Morrow, Robert E. Kopp, and Jerry X. Mitrovica, "Probabilistic Reanalysis of Twentieth-

Century Sea-Level Rise," *Nature* 517 (2015): 481–84.

14 Andrew C. Kemp, Benjamin P. Horton, Christopher H. Vane, Christopher E. Bernhardt, D. Reide Corbett, Simon E. Engelhart, Shimon C. Anisfeld, Andrew C. Parnell, and Niamh Cahill, "Sea-Level Change During the Last 2500 Years in New Jersey, USA," *Quaternary Science Reviews* 81 (2013): 90–104.

15 Simon E. Engelhart and Benjamin P. Horton, "Holocene Sea Level Database for the Atlantic Coast of the United States," *Quaternary Science Reviews* 54 (2012): 12–25.

16 Rita Zorn Moonsammy, David Steven Cohen, Lorraine E. Williams, *Pinelands Folklife* (New Brunswick, NJ: Rutgers University Press, 1987).

17 Kenneth G. Miller, Peter J. Sugarman, James V. Browning, Benjamin P. Horton, Alissa Stanley, Alicia Kahn, Jane Uptegrove, and Michael Aucott, "Sea-Level Rise in New Jersey over the Past 5000 Years: Implications to Anthropogenic Changes," *Global and Planetary Change* 66 (2009): 10–18; Andrew C. Kemp, et al., "Sea-Level Change During the Last 2500 Years in New Jersey, USA."

18 Benjamin P. Horton, Simon E. Engelhart, David F. Hill, Andrew C. Kemp, Daria Nikitina, Kenneth G. Miller, and W. Richard Peltier, "Influence of Tidal-Range Change and Sediment Compaction on Holocene Relative Sea-Level Change in New Jersey, USA," *Journal of Quaternary Science* 28 (2013): 403–11.

19 Robert E. Kopp, Andrew C. Kemp, Klaus Bittermann, Benjamin P. Horton, Jeffrey P. Donnelly, W. Roland Gehrels, Carling C. Hay, Jerry X. Mitrovica, Eric D. Morrow, and Stefan Rahmstorf, "Temperature-Driven Global Sea-Level Variability in the Common Era," *Proceedings of the National Academy of Sciences* (2016): E1434-41.

20 *Newark Evening News*, February 26, 1954.

21 Robert E. Kopp et al, "Temperature-Driven Global Sea-Level Variability in the Common Era."

ADDITIONAL REFERENCES

Murray F. Buell, "Time of Origin of New Jersey Pine Barrens Bogs," *Bulletin of the Torrey Botanical Club* 7, no. 2 (1970): 105–108. (See references included)

Calvin J. Heusser, "Vegetational History of the Pine Barrens," *Pine Barrens: Ecosystem and Landscapes*, ed. Richard T. T. Forman (New York: Academic Press, 1979), 215–27.

Karl F. Nordstrom, Nancy L. Jackson, and Charles T. Roman, "Facilitating Landform Migration by Removing Shore Protection Structures: Opportunities and Constraints," *Environmental Science and Policy* 66 (2016): 217–26.

Alfred C. Redfield, "The Ontogeny of a Salt Marsh Estuary," *Estuaries*, ed. G. H. Lauff (Washington, D.C.: American Association for the Advancement of Science, Publication No. 83, 1967), 108–114.

Alfred C. Redfield and Meyer Rubin, "The Age of Salt Marsh Peat and its Relation to Recent Changes in Sea Level at Barnstable, Massachusetts," *Proceeds of the National Academy of Science* 48, no. 10 (1962): 1728–35.

Charles T. Roman, Ralph E. Good, and Silas Little, "Ecology of Atlantic White Cedar Swamps in the New Jersey Pinelands," *Wetland Ecology and Management: Case Studies*, eds. D. F. Whigham, R. E. Good, J. Kvet (Netherlands: Kluwer Academic Publications, 1990), 163–73.

Simon E. Engelhart and Benjamin P. Horton, "Holocene Sea Level Database for the Atlantic Coast of the United States," *Quaternary Science Reviews* 54 (2012): 12–25.

Robert E. Kopp, Radley M. Horton, Christopher M. Little, Jerry X. Mitrovica, Michael Oppenheimer, D. J. Rasmussen, Benjamin H. Strauss, and Claudia Tebaldi. "Probabilistic 21st and 22nd Century Sea-Level Projections at a Global Network of Tide-Gauge Sites," *Earth's Future*, 2 (2014): 383–406.

Scull's portable steam saw. South Jersey's outer coastal plain has undergone deforestation and reforestation numerous times since Europeans first arrived. From the beginning, sawyers sought out the stands of Atlantic white cedar for the building products they yielded, ranging from clapboards to shingles. The first crude sawmills operated with waterpower, but as portable boilers became available during the mid-nineteenth century, sawyers could take their mill apparatus to the timber and relocate the machinery after the crew clear-cut all usable trees in one stand. Scull's portable steam sawmill, shown here operating on Zion Road in Egg Harbor Township, provides an indication on the arrangement of these mills. The horizontal boiler and its mounted engine rolled on wheels when pulled by horses. In this view, those wheels were removed and lay against a log on the ground on the right side of the image. The crew, which appear to be all African American, are producing clapboards. As sawyers depleted cedar of a usable size, they would often cut dead cedar, viewing them as "pre-seasoned," although the heartwood proved to be the densest part of the log.

A February Freshet & Breach in the Bank

Dallas Lore Sharp

FOREWORD

Dallas Lore Sharp, naturalist, writer, academic, and sometime South Jersey resident, was born in 1870 in Haleyville, Cumberland County, New Jersey. Sharp successfully communicated his appreciation for the natural world in essay collections such as *The Whole Year Round* (1915). Selected essays from this work were republished by the South Jersey Culture & History Center under the title *Seasons* in 2014.

Sharp's youth was spent amid the forest, fields, and swamps of Cumberland County, and his writing describes, with a keen eye and ready wit, the natural beauty of the area. He provides glimpses of nature that readers would need to leave the comfort of homes to find, and he encourages them to do so. Yet even sedentary readers can appreciate, through his writing, the beauty and mystery of nature, as well as local legends and real-life stories of area residents.

In a letter quoted in the *Bridgeton Evening News* in 1911, Sharp provides a brief autobiographical sketch that displays some of the gentle humor and contemplativeness found throughout his writing:

> I was born on a farm, and have lived close to the open country all my life.
>
> I was one of seven children, and only four years old when my father died, leaving my mother with the whole family to bring up.
>
> She did it. God bless her—a bringing up that, perhaps, is the most important thing in my life, for she made us as happy a home as seven children ever had; she made life keen and purposeful for us; she lived before us daily the "high emprise" she would have us undertake.
>
> She is a Quaker, and by her, not by the poet, I was early taught that the "groves were God's first temples." She gave me the liberty of the fields, after teaching me how to pray.
>
> I was about eighteen when I wrote my first essay for *The Youth's Companion*; twenty-one when I entered Brown University; twenty-five when I was married; thirty-one when my first book and my first boy were born.
>
> Now I am forty, with only four books and only four boys to my credit. I hoped there might be eight, for there is room enough and apples enough in the cellar this winter. (It has been a good apple year.)
>
> Only four! I must fall back upon the thought that, after all, it is quality, not mere quantity, that counts. Still, there were seven of us.[1]

The two essays reprinted here, "A February Freshet" and "A Breach in the Bank," recount the tale of a spring thaw along the Maurice River. Freshets, or late spring melts accompanied by heavy rains and fierce winds, brought the danger of flooding, disastrous to farmers' fields and low-lying towns. Any meadowlands along the river that were not protected by banks flooded during these storms. Farmers in the vicinity of Mauricetown, Leesburg, Port Norris, and Port Elizabeth built and patrolled banks in an attempt to protect the land. The seasonal storms began with heavy showers followed by incredible gusts of winds. One result was downed trees and branches that littered fields and muddy town sidewalks alike.[2]

"A February Freshet" serves as prelude to "A Breach in the Bank," describing the bank to protect the meadows along the Maurice River, the shore meadows, and the impact of freshets. "A Breach in the Bank" is the tale of a young boy, patrolling the banks during a tremendous storm, who discovers a growing breach within one of them. Sharp's older brother, Joseph B. Sharp, is the model for the essay's hero, having dealt, in his youth, with several such breaches in the banks of the Maurice River.[3]

This tale of bravery also describes the actions of the goodly Doctor Sam, Dr. Samuel Butcher (1838–1901) of Mauricetown. Samuel was one of several Butchers who practiced medicine in the area from the second quarter of the nineteenth century well into the second half of the twentieth century. Lisa E. Cox, Edward Hutton, and Ruth Hutton-William's article in *SoJourn* 1.2, "From Butcher Knife to Scalpel: Four Generations of South Jersey Physicians," chronicles the career of these important South Jersey physicians.

Together, both stories demonstrate Sharp's commitment to the preservation of nature through his descriptive prose of the local South Jersey landscape. He presents the beautiful, if unpredictable, shore meadowlands of South Jersey with great emotional impact.

Kent Mattia

A February Freshet

One of the very interesting events in my out-of-door year is the February freshet. Perhaps you call it the February thaw. That is all it could be called this year; and, in fact, a thaw is all that it ever is for me, nowadays, living, as I do, high and dry here, on Mullein Hill,[4] above a sputtering little trout brook that could not have a freshet if it tried.

But Maurice River could have a freshet without trying. Let the high south winds, the high tides, and the warm spring rains come on together, let them drive in hard for a day and a night, as I have known them to do, and the deep, dark river goes mad! The tossing tide sweeps over the wharves, swirls about the piles of the great bridge, leaps foaming into the air, and up and down its long high banks beats with all its wild might to break through into the fertile meadows below.

There are wider rivers, and other, more exciting things, than spring freshets; but there were not when I was a boy. Why, Maurice River was so wide that there was but a single boy in the town, as I remember, who could stand at one end of the draw-bridge and skim an oyster-shell over to the opposite end! The best that I could do was to throw my voice across and hear it echo from the long, hollow barn on the other bank. It would seem to me to strike the barn in the middle, leap from end to end like a creature caged, and then bound back to me faint and frightened from across the dark tide.

I feared the river. Oh, but I loved it, too. Its tides were always rising or falling—going down to the Delaware Bay and on to the sea. And in from the bay, or out to the bay, with white sails set, the big boats were always moving. And when they had gone, out over the wide water the gulls or the fish hawks would sail, or a great blue heron, with wings like the fans of an old Dutch mill, would beat ponderously across.

I loved the river. I loved the sound of the calking-maul and the adze in the shipyard, and the smell of the

The Maurice River and its iron swing bridge at Mauricetown, ca. 1907. *Courtesy of the Mickey Smith collection.*

chips and tarred oakum; the chatter of the wrens among the reeds and calamus; the pink of the mallow and wild roses along the high mud banks; the fishy ditches with their deep sluiceways through the bank into the river; and the vast, vast tide-marshes that, to this day, seem to me to stretch way to the very edge of the world.

What a world for a boy to drive cows into every morning and drive them home from every night, as I used to help do! Or to trap muskrats in during the winter; to go fishing in during the summer; to go splashing up and down in when the great February freshet came on!

For of all the events of the year, none had such fascination for me as the high winds and warm downpour that flooded the wharves, that drove the men of the village out to guard the river-banks, and that drowned out of their burrows and winter hiding-places all the wild things that lived within reach of the spreading tide.

The drawings that accompany this text are by Robert Bruce Horsfall, and adorned the first edition of Sharp's *The Whole Year Round*.

The water would pour over the meadows and run far back into the swamps and farm lands, setting everything afloat that could float—rails, logs, branches; upon which, as chance offered, some struggling creature would crawl, and drift away to safety.

But not always to safety; for over the meadows the crows and fish hawks, gulls, herons, bitterns, and at night the owls, were constantly beating to pounce upon the helpless voyagers, even taking the muskrats an easy prey, through their weakness from exposure and long swimming in the water.

There would be only two shores to this wild meadow-sea—the river-bank, a mere line of earth drawn through the water, and the distant shore of the upland. If the wind blew from the upland toward the bank, then the drift would all set that way, and before long a multitude of shipwrecked creatures would be tossed upon this narrow breakwater, that stood, a bare three feet of clay, against the wilder river-sea beyond.

To walk up and down the bank then was like entering a natural history museum where all the specimens

were alive; or like going to a small menagerie. Sparrows, finches, robins, mice, moles, voles, shrews, snakes, turtles, squirrels, muskrats, with even a mink and an opossum now and then, would scurry from beneath your feet or dive back into the water as you passed along.

And by what strange craft they sometimes came! I once saw two muskrats and a gray squirrel floating along on the top of one of the muskrats' houses. And again a little bob-tailed meadow mouse came rocking along in a drifting catbird's nest which the waves had washed from its anchorage in the rosebushes. And out on the top of some tall stake, or up among the limbs of a tree you would see little huddled bunches of fur, a muskrat perhaps that had never climbed before in his life, waiting, like a sailor lashed to the rigging, to be taken off.

But it was not the multitude of wild things—birds, beasts, insects—that fascinated me most, that led me out along the slippery, dangerous bank through the swirling storm; it was rather the fear and confusion of the animals, the wild giant-spirit raging over the face of the earth and sky, daunting and terrifying them, that drew me.

Many of the small creatures had been wakened by the flood out of their deep winter sleep, and, dazed and numbed and frightened, they seemed to know nothing, to care for nothing but the touch of the solid earth to their feet.

All of their natural desires and instincts, their hatreds, hungers, terrors, were sunk beneath the waters. They had lost their wits, like human creatures in a panic, and, struggling, fighting for a foothold, they did not notice me unless I made at them, and then only took to the water a moment to escape the instant peril.

The sight was strange, as if this were another planet and not our orderly, peaceful world at all. Nor, indeed, was it; for fear cowered everywhere, in all the things that were of the earth, as over the earth and everything upon it raged the fury of river and sky.

The frail mud bank trembled under the beating of the waves; the sunken sluices strangled and shook deep down through the whirlpools sucking at their

This view is looking down the Maurice River towards its confluence with Delaware Bay from Mauricetown, located on the west shore of the waterway. The meadows just beyond the town, stretching to the horizon, featured protective banks to keep the river from flooding the wetlands, thereby making this area agriculturally productive. *From a glass-plate negative, courtesy of the Mickey Smith collection.*

mouths; the flocks of scattered sea-birds—ducks and brant—veered into sight, dashed down toward the white waters or drove over with mad speed, while the winds screamed and the sky hung black like a torn and flapping sail.

And I, too, would have to drop upon all fours, with the mice and muskrats, and cling to the bank for my life, as the snarling river, leaping at me, would plunge clear over into the meadow below.

A winter blizzard is more deadly, but not more fearful, nor so wild and tumultuous. For in such a storm as this the foundations of the deep seem to be broken up, the frame of the world shaken, and you, and the mice, and the muskrats, share alike the wild, fierce spirit and the fear.

To be out in such a storm, out where you can feel its full fury, as upon a strip of bank in the midst of the churning waters, is good for one. To experience a common peril with your fellow mortals, though they be only mice and muskrats, is good for one; for it is to share by so much in their humble lives, and by so much to live outside of one's own little self.

And then again, we are so accustomed to the order and fair weather of our part of the globe, that we get to feel as if the universe were being particularly managed for us; nay, that we, personally, are managing the universe. To flatten out on a quaking ridge of earth or be blown into the river; to hear no voice but the roar of the storm, and to have no part or power in the mighty tumult of such a storm, makes one feel about the size of a mouse, makes one feel how vast is the universe, and how fearful the vortex of its warring forces!

The shriek of those winds is still in my ears, the sting of the driving rains still on my face, the motion of that frail mud bank, swimming like a long sea-serpent in the swirling waters, I can still feel to my finger-tips. And the growl of the river, the streaming shreds of the sky, the confusion beneath and about me, the mice and muskrats clinging with me for a foothold—I live it all again at the first spatter of a February rain upon my face.

To be out in a February freshet, out in a big spring break-up, is to get a breaking up one's self, a preparation, like Nature's, for a new lease of life—for spring.

A February Freshet & Breach in the Bank

A Breach in the Bank

The February freshet had come. We had been expecting it, but no one along Maurice River had ever seen so wild and warm and ominous a spring storm as this. So sudden and complete a break-up of winter no one could remember; nor so high a tide, so rain-thick and driving a south wind. It had begun the night before, and now, along near noon, the river and meadows were a tumult of white waters, with the gale so strong that one could hardly hold his own on the drawbridge that groaned from pier to pier in the grip of the maddened storm.

It was into the teeth of this gale that a small boy dressed in large yellow "oil-skins" made his slow way out along the narrow bank of the river toward the sluices that controlled the tides of the great meadows.

The boy was in the large yellow oil-skins; not dressed, no, for he was simply inside of them, his feet and hands and the top of his head having managed to work their way out. It seems, at least, that his head was partly out, for on the top of the oil-skins sat a large black sou'wester. And in the arms of the oil-skins lay an old army musket, so big and long that it seemed to be walking away with the oil-skins, as the oil-skins seemed to be walking away with the boy.

I can feel the kick of that old musket yet, and the prick of the dried sand-burs among which she knocked me. I can hear the rough rasping of the chafing legs of those oil-skins too, though I was not the boy this time inside of them. But I knew the boy who was, a real boy; and I know that he made his careful way along the trembling river-bank out into the sunken meadows, meadows that later on I saw the river burst into and claim—and it still claims them, as I saw only last summer, when after thirty years of absence I once more

stood at the end of that bank looking over a watery waste which was once the richest of farm lands.

Never, it seemed, had the village known such wind and rain and such a tide. It was a strange, wild scene from the drawbridge—wharves obliterated, river white with flying spume and tossing ice-cakes, the great bridge swaying and shrieking in the wind, and over everything the blur of the swirling rain.

The little figure in yellow oil-skins was not the only one that had gone along the bank since morning, for a party of men had carefully inspected every foot of the bank to the last sluice, for fear that there might be a weak spot somewhere. Let a breach occur with such a tide as this and it could never be stopped.

And now, somewhat past noon, the men were again upon the bank. As they neared Five-Forks sluice, the central and largest of the water-gates, they heard a smothered boom above the scream of the wind in their ears. They were startled; but it was only the sound of a gun somewhere off in the meadow. It was the gun of the boy in the oil-skins.

Late that afternoon Doctor "Sam," driving home along the flooded road of the low back swamp, caught sight, as he came out in view of the river, of a little figure in yellow oil-skins away out on the meadow.

The doctor stopped his horse and hallooed. But the boy did not hear. The rain on his coat, the wind and the river in his ears drowned every other sound.

The dusk was falling, and as the doctor looked out over the wild scene, he put his hands to his mouth and called again. The yellow figure had been blotted out by the rain. There was no response, and the doctor drove on.

Meanwhile the boy in the yellow oil-skins was splashing slowly back along the narrow, slippery clay bank. He was wet, but he was warm, and he loved the roar of the wind and the beat of the driving rain.

As the mist and rain were fast mixing with the dusk of the twilight, he quickened his steps. His path in places was hardly a foot wide, covered with rose and elder bushes mostly; but bare in spots where holes and low worn stretches had been recently built up with cubes of the tough blue mud of the flats.

The tide was already even with the top of the bank and was still rising. It leaped and hit at his feet as he picked his way along. The cakes of white ice crunched and heeled up against the bank with here and there one flung fairly across his path. The tossing water frequently splashed across. Twice he jumped places where the tide was running over down into the meadows below.

How quickly the night had come! It was dark when he reached Five-Forks sluice—the middle point in the long, high bank. While still some distance off he heard the sullen roar of the big sluice, through which the swollen river was trying to force its way.

He paused to listen a moment. He knew the peculiar voice of every one of these gateways, as he knew every foot of the river-bank.

There was nothing wrong with the sullen roar. But how deep and threatening! He could feel the sound even better than he could hear it, far down below him. He started forward, to pass on, when he half felt, through the long, regular throbbing of the sluice, a shorter, faster, closer quiver, as of a small running stream in the bank very near his feet.

Dropping quickly to his knees, he laid his ear to the wet earth. A cold, black hand seemed to seize upon him. He heard the purr of running water!

It must be down about three feet. He could distinctly feel it tearing through.

Without rising he scrambled down the meadow side of the bank to see the size of the breach. He could hear nothing of it for the boiling at the gates of the sluice. It was so dark he could scarcely see. But near the bottom the mud suddenly caved beneath his feet, and a rush of cold water caught at his knees.

The hole was greater than he feared.

Crawling back to the top of the bank, he leaned out over the river side. A large cake of ice hung in water in front of him. He pushed it aside and, bending until his face barely cleared the surface of the river, he discovered a small sucking eddy, whose swirling hole he knew ran into the breach.

He edged farther out and reached down under the water and touched the upper rim of the hole. How large might it be? Swinging round, he dug his fingers into the bank and lowered himself feet first until he stood in the hole. It was the size of a small bucket, but he could almost feel it going beneath his feet, and a sudden terror took hold upon him.

He was only a boy, and the dark night, the wild river, the vast, sweeping storm, the roar and tremor and tumult flattened him for a moment to the ridge of the bank in a panic of fear!

But he heard the water running, he felt the bank going directly beneath where he lay, and getting to his feet he started for the village. A single hasty step and, but for the piles of the sluice, he would have plunged into the river.

He must feel his way; but he never could do it in time to save the bank. The breach must be stopped at once. He must stop it and keep it stopped until the next patrol brought help.

Feeling his way back, he dropped again upon his hands and knees above the breach to think for moment.

The cake of ice hung as before in the eddy. Catching it, he tipped it and thrust it down across the mouth of the hole, but it slipped from his cold fingers and dived away. He pushed down the butt of his musket, turned it flat, but it was not broad enough to cover the opening. Then he lowered himself again, and stood in it, wedging the musket in between his boots; but he could feel the water still tearing through at the sides, and eating all the faster.

He clambered back to the top of the bank, put his hand to his mouth and shouted. The only answer was the scream of the wind and the cry of a brant passing overhead.

Then the boy laughed. "Easy enough," he muttered, and, picking up the musket, he leaned once more out over the river and thrust the steel barrel of the gun hard into the mud just below the hole. Then, stepping easily down, he sat squarely into the breach, the gun like a stake in front of him sticking up between his knees.

Then he laughed again, as he caught his breath, for he had squeezed into the hole like a stopper into a bottle, his big oil-skins filling the breach completely.

The water stood above the middle of his breast, and the tide was still rising. Darkness had now settled, but the ghostly ice-cakes, tipping, slipping toward him, were spectral white. He had to shove them back as now and then one rose before his face. The sky was black, and the deep water below him was blacker. And how cold it was!

Doctor Sam had been stopped by the flooded roads on his way home, and lights shone in the windows as he entered the village. He turned a little out of his way and halted in front of a small cottage near the bridge.

"Is Joe here?" he asked.

"No," answered the mother; "he went down the meadow for muskrats and has not returned yet. He's probably over with the men at the store."

Doctor Sam drove on to the store.

There was no boy in yellow oil-skins in the store.

Doctor Sam picked up a lighted lantern.

"Come on," he said. "I'm wet, but I want a look at those sluices," and started for the river, followed immediately by the men, whom he led in single file out along the bank.

Swinging his lantern low, he pushed into the teeth of the gale at a pace that left the line of lights straggling far behind.

"What a night!" he growled. "If I had a boy of my own—" and he threw the light as far as he could over the seething river and then down over the flooded meadow.

Ahead he heard the roar of Five-Forks sluice, and swung his lantern high, as if to signal it, so like the rush of a coming train was the sound of the waters.

But the little engineer in yellow oil-skins could not see the signal. He had almost ceased to watch. With his arm cramped about his gun, he was still at his post; but the ice-cakes floated in and touched him; the water no longer felt cold.

On this side, then on that, out over the swollen river, down into the tossing meadow flared the lantern as the doctor worked his way along.

Above the great sluice he paused a moment, then bent his head to the wind and started on, when his foot touched something soft that yielded strangely, sending a shiver over him, and his light fell upon a bunch of four dead muskrats lying in the path.

Along the meadow side flashed the lantern, up and over the riverside, and Doctor Sam, reaching quickly down, drew a limp little form in yellow oil-skins out of the water, as the men behind him came up.

A gurgle, a hiss, a small whirlpool sucking at the surface,—and the tide was again tearing through the breach that the boy had filled.

The men sprang quickly to their task, and did it well, while Doctor Sam, shielding the limp little form from the wind, forced a vial of something between the white lips, saying over to himself as he watched the closed eyes open, "If I had a boy of my own—If I had a boy—"

. . . .

No, Doctor Sam never had a boy of his own; but he always felt, I think, that the boy of those yellow oil-skins was somehow pretty nearly his.

. . . .

After a long, cold winter how I love the spatter on my face of the first February rain! The little trout brook below me foams and sometimes overruns the road, and as its small noise ascends the hill, I can hear—the wind on a great river, the wash of waves against a narrow bank, and the muffled roar of quaking sluices as when a February freshet is on.

About the Editor

Kent Mattia is a Monmouth County resident, an avid creative writer and Literature student at Stockton University, and the current Co-Editor-In-Chief of *Stockpot Literary Magazine*.

Endnotes

1 "An Apostle of Good Cheer," *Bridgeton Evening News* (Bridgeton, NJ), March 9, 1911, 4. The quotation "Grove's were God's first temples," is from the opening of "A Forest Hymn," a poem by William Cullen Bryant.

2 "The Big Tide," *Bridgeton Evening News* (Bridgeton, NJ), February 19, 1896, 4.

3 "'Winter' By Dallas Lore Sharp," *Bridgeton Evening News* (Bridgeton, NJ), July 15, 1912, 4.

4 Dallas Lore Sharp lived at Mullein Hill, on a fourteen-acre farm in Hingam, Massachusetts. He published a series of essays describing his life in the place entitled *The Hills of Hingham* (Boston: Houghton Mifflin Company, 1916). Here is a portion of the first paragraph, replete with Sharp's dry, understated wit: "Really there are no hills in Hingham, to speak of, except Bradley Hill and Peartree Hill and Turkey Hill, and Otis and Planter's and Prospect Hills, Hingham being more noted for its harbor and plains. Everybody has heard of Hingham smelts. Mullein Hill is in Hingham, too, but Mullein Hill is only a wrinkle on the face of Liberty Plain, which accounts partly for our having it. Almost anybody can have a hill in Hingham who is content without elevation, a surveyor's term as applied to hills, and a purely accidental property which is not at all essential to real hillness, or the sense of height. We have a stump on Mullein Hill for height" (*The Hills of Hingham*, 1–2).

Call for Articles

The South Jersey Culture & History Center at Stockton University publishes twice yearly issues of *SoJourn*. We actively seek community members, avocational historians, and scholars to contribute essays on topics related to South Jersey. Illustrations to accompany these articles will be a plus. Articles should be written for laypersons who are interested and curious about South Jersey topics, but do not necessarily have expertise in the areas covered. Potential authors should check SJCHC's website for a link to a simplified style sheet guide for article preparation—www.stockton.edu/sjchc/—or just follow the style in this issue. Journal editors will be happy to guide any would-be authors. In certain instances, Stockton editing interns may be assigned to help research topics and/or assist authors with writing.

Sample topics might include:
Biographical sketches of important but forgotten local people; the development or succession of a community's roads, bridges or buildings; local transportation (focused by mode, area or era) and what changes it wrought in the served communities; history of community businesses and industries (wineries, garment factories, agriculture, boat building, clamming, etc.); old school houses, old hotels, or meeting halls; narrative descriptions of local geographical features; essays concerned with folklore, music, arts; and reviews of new local interest publications. Photo essays and old photograph and postcard reproductions are welcome with applicable captions. In short, if a South Jersey topic interests you, it will likely interest *SoJourn*'s readers.

Parameters for submissions:
• Submissions must pertain to topics bounded within the eight southernmost counties of New Jersey (Burlington & Ocean Counties and south)
• Manuscripts should be approximately 3,000–4,000 words long (5 to 7 pages of single-spaced text and 9 to 12 pages including images)
• Manuscripts should conform to the *SoJourn* style sheet, available here: https://blogs.stockton.edu/sjchc/sojourn-style-sheet/
• Manuscripts, if at all possible, should be submitted in digital format (Word- or pdf-formatted documents preferred)
• Images should be submitted as high-resolution tiff- or jpeg-formatted files (editors can assist with digital conversion of photos if necessary). 300 dpi resolution, or higher, preferred
• Complete and appropriate citations printed as endnotes should be employed (see style sheet)
• Original submissions only. Copyright licenses for all images must be obtained by the author or should be copyright-free figures and/or figures in the public domain
• If essays are accepted, authors should submit a short 50 to 100 word autobiographical statement
• Articles need to be more than just a chronology of the given topic. The author should be able to properly contextualize the subject by answering such questions as: a) why is this important?; b) what is the impact on the local or regional history? and c) how does it compare to similar events/personages/changes/processes in other localities?

Call for submissions:
Submissions for winter issues are due before September 1; for summer issues, January 15. Send inquiries or submissions to Thomas.Kinsella@stockton.edu or Paul.Schopp@stockton.edu.

Notes and Queries: Finally, we invite readers to submit brief notes of interest or queries about topics of South Jersey history to either of the two editors named immediately above.